This Pulse of Life,
These Words
I Found

This Pulse of Life,
These Words
I Found

Miguel Ángel Olivé Iglesias

First Edition

Wet Ink Books
www.WetInkBooks.com
WetInkBooks@gmail.com

This Pulse of Life, These Words I Found
by Miguel Ángel Olivé Iglesias

Cover Image – Richard M. Grove
Cover Design – Richard M. Grove
Layout and Design – Richard M. Grove

Typeset in Garamond
Printed and bound in Canada
Distributed in USA by Ingram,
    – to set up an account – 1-800-937-0152

Library and Archives Canada Cataloguing in Publication

Title: This pulse of life, these words I found / Miguel Ángel Olivé Iglesias.
Names: Olivé Iglesias, Miguel Ángel, 1965- author. |
        Olivé Iglesias, Miguel Ángel, 1965- Poems.
    Selections. | Olivé Iglesias, Miguel Ángel, 1965- Poems. Selections. English.
Description: Poems. | Includes previously published poems. |
        Poems in English with Spanish translation.
Identifiers: Canadiana (print) 20220203431 |
        Canadiana (ebook) 20220203555 |
        ISBN 9781989786680 (softcover) | ISBN 9781989786697 (ebook)
Classification: LCC PR9240.9.O55 A2 2022 | DDC 811/.6—dc23

Acknowledgements

I thank God and The Virgin for all the blessings in my life. I have prayed for me, my family, my friends, and I have been listened to. I have prayed for peace of mind, goodness, health, fortitude. He has always smiled on me, she has been always kind. That is why I live in trust, certainty and gratefulness. I cannot ask for more. Theirs is the best pulse of life, the best source for words.

I thank Amanda, my daughter, who lights up my life in so many ways. I still marvel how I could even breathe before she was born.

I will always be deeply in debt with Jorge Alberto Pérez Hernández, Manuel Velázquez, Richard Grove, James Deahl and John B. Lee, all of them honorable pillars of the Canada Cuba Literary Alliance (CCLA). They are also writers and editors, who encouraged me to write poetry and expand my themes. Reading their poetry and listening to their valuable advice paved the way towards my own style.

Saying names is risky: you leave some out. So, I thank **every** Cuban and Canadian poet, CCLA member and non-member, I have had the pleasure to read these last four years. Their combined influences touch my poems. If *any* of my poems are *any* good, I owe it to my poet friends; if none is, it is only *my* fault!

This second book is here today thanks to them. It turned into a paper book once more thanks to Tai. He put his efforts, budget, trust and love into it. I still don´t have enough words – English, Spanish or any other language – to show Tai, and them all, my profound gratitude.

I especially thank Alina, my wife, for her support and hours of self-imposed silence so I could flirt with my muses and write my humble pieces.

To my mother,
in memoriam
How I wish
you could read my poems!

To those who will always be my pillars:

The family I was born into and lived with:
my mother, my father, my sister.
They are the first pillar, the seed, the forge, the impulse.

The family I created, Amanda,
and the family life led me to: Alina, Alianna, Ahitana.
They are the second pillar, the reason to go on,
the light at the end of the tunnel.

The family we choose (or are chosen by):
my Cuban and Canadian friends – so many.
The third pillar, the support, the shelter.

Table of Contents

Introduction

In his poem, "The First Day," Miguel Ángel Olivé Iglesias clearly announces who he is as a poet when he writes, this is where I stand, before the primordial source.

That source, raw and genuine, goes right to the heart of his world and informs his aesthetics as a poet. It is elemental, essential, and thus, for Olivé, universal. Language accrues as incoming waves which he interprets as "ocean messages" that allow him to "breathe in the pulse of life." The poetry in this book comes from that core of experience— everyday life, everyday sorrows and joy, and, most significantly, from trying to make sense of love at its source. It is poetry about something or someone. There is a release of emotions in his writing that engineers a bridge between himself and his subjects and it's a bridge that his readers can easily cross.

Olivé calls himself a romantic. I don't doubt it. I would add "lyrical" to that epithet. There is evidence of the lyrical romantic in almost every poem in this collection. In "Rivers" lovers are "a river of two surging/towards the finish." Even the seasons take on a metaphoric life as desire and physical love in the poem "Of Your Seasons" where "Winter has generously frozen/time/in your flesh" and "Summer brings tides of heat,/it comes nude …." Another poet, Li Po, more ancient, more remote than Olivé, wrote about his broken heart in a letter to a distant friend:

> If only I were free of life
> that I may write of life
> as I am now free of love.

The paradox is obvious, if not profound. Poetry requires a degree of detachment which allows for a self-consciousness that imposes rigour and a guiding structure to the writing. We call that form, and it gives the poem direction beyond the content or subject matter. Together, that combination of form and content make the poem an integrated, unified whole, allowing themes to flourish, ideas to bounce, devices to intrigue. Olivé manipulates these to his advantage. His diction and syntax speak the language of love, confront the obstacles of the quotidian. His themes are the broad brushstrokes we often find in a romantic—life, love, fear of falling, the roaring sea, sun-drenched clouds, the taste of lips, a ticking watch that's stopped—informing both his images and his perspective on the "I" that is at the centre of these poems.

As a whole, it would be easy to categorize this collection as lyrical love poems. There is no question that many of these poems present themselves as Valentine's Day gone the way of Groundhog Day, as the movie of the same name so entertainingly immortalized in popular culture. The theme of love is on a recurring cycle. But there is more to Olivé' poetry than a bleeding heart dripping ink-stained sentiments.

I often consider poetry as a form of visual art painted with words. As varied as that world of art can be with paintings ranging from the representational to the abstract, so too poetry encompasses such variety. The surreal and the absurd in poetry can be as intellectually effective as a Dali or painting by Frida Kahlo. In my mind, Picasso's Guernica is an epic poem like no other, and there are poems by Ashbery I consider echoes of the finest cubist paintings. Such parallels are endless. The image often dominates a poem's aesthetics. As I read this book I saw several poems as watercolours and small pastels where the edges have been blurred or the light dimmed and softened to strike a mood or suggest the immaterial. Some are highly visual poems, meant to be seen as much as heard:

> Darkening skycanvas looms
> beyond the window
> fistfuls of angry clouds float windward
> as hearts on earth leap
> uncertain ("Even in the Rain")

The image is striking, almost Turner-like in scope, a "skycanvas," no less, that Olivé has contained and framed in a tight pastel I'd love to put up on my wall. In another poem, "Raingift," Olivé sees the "gift of transparency" in "a sky bathed in light," a watercolour of intimate proportions which the poet himself recognizes as a "collage of light/and my tropes."

There are many pleasant surprises in this collection, poems that call to the reader in a voice that is tender, personal, honest, heartfelt and sincere—poems that ask to be heard because Olivé is as much an auditory poet as he is visual. And once they are heard and then visualized in the mind's eye, these poems become entities with a life of their own. They breathe, and breathing, they take on a pulse of life that Olivé, the romantic, the lyric poet, has given them.

Antony Di Nardo
Canadian poet and teacher

Preface by the Author

This Pulse of Life, These Words I Found, fills me in many ways. It is a result of the inevitable urge that led me to write in the first place more than thirty-five years ago, systematically publish with the Canada Cuba Literary Alliance (CCLA) and in other generous magazines like Canadian Stories, launch my first solo full-length poetry book with Hidden Brook Press, Forge of Words (2020), and present this one now.

The title is a blend of lines from two of my poems. I feel they capture the essence of what I write about: life, love, poetry, family, people, nature, circumstances, events. They are a unique motivation that invades me and I have modestly and gratefully turned into poetry thanks to that pulse of life and those words I found. It was gratifying to read similar lines a few months ago in a poem by Malca Litovitz and Elana Wolff, "Pulse."

My writing is because many good friends have helped me grow as a humble poet. They have painstakingly carved poetry in me, paved the way to publication and supported me, making my poems "passable/publishable" and respectful towards the readership, Canadian, Cuban or beyond. Many old and new poet friends who have taught me English, composing, style and a growing awareness of things around me I had not taken notice of before I met them. James Deahl was so right when he said: "No poet learns the craft without help and sage advice from those who have already achieved a higher level of writing." (Taken from Under the Mulberry Tree: Poems for & about Raymond Souster. Quattro Books Inc. 2014. Edited by James Deahl)

In a review I wrote on James Deahl's Even This Land Was Born Of Light, I said that "Poets have a gift: they provide light, a different one. They craft words and images in ways no one else can and lay them down for us to marvel at a world that had been there but we hadn´t noticed." Poets I read teach me that every day.

Merle Amodeo says in her poem, "Ode to Poetry," that "you will find the spirit of the poem" and asks us to "Let the poem weave its magic." This Pulse of Life, These Words I Found is about this. The revelation of the spirit that makes a poem take flight, of the themes pulsing in the outside world where life is in the making, of the magic that we can see with poet eyes then take and weave into words. "Love, family… nature are at the soul of his poems." These are words by Richard Marvin Grove (Tai), CCLA Founding President. He referred to my poems in The Bridges Series book IV, Where the Heart Lies (2018), but I am so proud they equally apply to my poems in This Pulse of Life, These Words I Found.

John B. Lee said: "I want the heart to feel true sentiment… the body to come alive… the soul to thrill… and the spirit to surround and be surrounded." I have always felt this way when I write my poems. I have always enjoyed, lived, suffered and trembled writing poetry. That is a start, timid, humble, but a start. From where I stand, where I live, I am influenced by that higher aura poets have, and I have tried to write accordingly inspired by them. Elana Wolff's answer in an interview best describes my words: "Inspiration comes by looking closely, seeing deeply, reading (and misreading) the work of other poets, living my life, thinking and feeling. Inspiration comes even through sleep and dreaming. Poetry, for me, is linked to an open way of being in the world—so inspiration can come from anywhere, at any time."

Side by side my new poems, I included poems I had previously published in separate issues and periodicals. They are favorites I love keeping close to me and wanted to have them together in one book. While reading me, please keep in mind two things: one, I am not an English-speaking/writing poet; two, I am not even a poet! I am a Cuban professor who loves English and writing poems; mostly in English.

The poems in this collection were originally felt and written in English (except "Today is a moment"); my heart and zeal remained Cuban though. Even when this is not an originally conceived, strictly bilingual edition, I decided to include a Spanish version of my poems for family, friends and a broader readership familiar only with Spanish. They deserve to partake in my own perceptions, measureless pleasure and possible success in sharing what I feel while writing.

I thank Tai, he knows how much, for the opportunity to make them public. I thank Jorge, my friend/brother, for his trust and his fostering, big-hearted words in the Afterword. Jorge is becoming sort of a follower of my writings! He almost persuaded me into believing I am a poet! But then I think of John B. Lee – yes, John B. Lee – saying that he'd "… far rather be referred to as someone who writes poetry than be called a poet." (Taken from John B. Lee's book This is How We See the World, Hidden Brook Press, 2017. His introductory words)

Thank you, readers, for taking time to read me for in reading this book you will read my poems and my whole self, my life pulses and the words I could muster to craft them.

to feel the pulse of life
Elana Wolff and Malca Litovitz

I am thankful when the muses visit
John B. Lee

poetry and I found each other
Richard Marvin Grove (Tai)

poems must always be born anew
James Deahl

This Pulse of Life,
These Words
I Found

complete

… a blank page I wrote
myself upon with words. Don Gutteridge
Words dancing. Ariadne Sawyer
This poem is a dance a ritual. John B. Lee

I am zapping words
into my PC screen
can´t help it when am inspired
no point in knowing now if
it's topnotch or unexceptional material
it just feels good to write

the door in front of me shows
an afternoon pasting dusks on
an ousted sun
that still glitters on butterflies nearby
– timid stars begin to shoot right through
a twilight mantle –

I am gratefully
crafting words,

no need to judge them now
I just feel complete

pleno

… una página en blanco sobre la que
me escribí yo mismo con palabras. Don Gutteridge
Palabras bailando. Ariadne Sawyer
Este poema es un baile un ritual. John B. Lee

estoy enviando palabras
a la pantalla de mi computadora
no puedo evitarlo cuando estoy inspirado
no tiene sentido saber ahora si
es material de primera o común
se siente sencillamente bien

la puerta frente a mí me muestra
una tarde que pega ocasos sobre
un desterrado sol
que aún brilla en mariposas cercanas
– tímidas estrellas comienzan a relucir a través
de un manto crepuscular –

estoy agradecidamente
tallando palabras,

no hay necesidad de juzgarlas ahora
me siento sencillamente pleno

Dance of Words

Words dancing. Ariadne Sawyer
This poem is a dance a ritual. John B. Lee

They lie, dormant,
waiting until the time is ripe

then they awaken
sway gently at first
grow wings, fly
onto blank spaces of paper
urging the pencil
nourished by life.

They follow their own rhythms
a ritual into the most fruitful of moments

in a dance
of poet
and words.

Danza de las palabras

Palabras bailando. Ariadne Sawyer
Este poema es un baile un ritual. John B. Lee

Reposan, latentes,
esperando hasta el momento oportuno

entonces despiertan
se mecen suavemente al principio
les nacen alas, se elevan
sobre blancos espacios de papel
incitando al lápiz
nutridas por la vida.

Siguen sus propios ritmos
un ritual hacia el más fértil de los momentos

en una danza
del poeta
y las palabras.

Wingcharm

... there you go – spinning your wings. Elana Wolff
... open like wings–unstoppable. Eva Kolacz

Winged letters flutter
like a hummingbird sipping in mid air
fidgety;

for a millionth of an instant she goes quiet
all goes quite

she perches, a miracle, pecks my hand –
I look,
 her flapping
leaves trembling words
on my notepad. Then

she flies back
to her nest but

the winged letters
stay with me.

Hechizo de alas

… ahí vas – haciendo girar tus alas. Elana Wolff
… abierto como alas–imparable. Eva Kolacz

Letras aladas revolotean
como un colibrí libando en vuelo
impaciente;

por una millonésima de un instante se aquieta
todo se aquieta

se posa, un milagro, picotea mi mano –
miro,
su aleteo
deja palabras temblorosas
sobre mi bloc de notas. Entonces

vuela de regreso
a su nido pero

las letras aladas
se quedan conmigo.

Magic of the Conch

To my daughter, Amanda, for August 2010

The sunniest of days rises over
the Gibara beach. My daughter and I ramble
leaving footprint art on the fickle sand
while water and earth openly consummate
on the shoreline their ancient undersea romance.
Look, Dad! - Skips my daughter joyfully, drawing
less artistic trails now - *A conch! That's a huge one!*
We approach the seashell. *Beautiful one*,
I tell her, *The ocean lives inside it, you can hear
it rumble within its spirals…*
What?! How?! - She asks. *Well, bring the conch near your ear,
close your eyes and listen, listen to the sea roll
and murmur, flow and rumble…*
She looks at me in half disbelief
but does as she is told. Her eyes light up
when she hears the magic of the conch. *Wow!!*
The sea is in there!! - She exclaims
giving me her smile,
the sunniest of smiles.

La magia de la concha

A mi hija, Amanda, por Agosto del 2010…

El más soleado de los días se levanta sobre
la playa de Gibara. Mi hija y yo paseamos
dejando arte de huellas en la veleidosa arena
mientras el agua y la tierra consuman abiertamente
en la orilla su antiguo idilio submarino.
¡Mira, Papá! - Salta mi hija jubilosamente, dibujando
rastros menos artísticos ahora - *¡Una concha! ¡Es enorme!*
Nos acercamos al caracol. *Hermosa,*
le digo, *El océano vive en su interior, se puede oír
su resonar dentro de sus espirales…*
¡¿Qué?! ¡¿Cómo?! - Me pregunta. *Bueno, acerca la concha a tu oído,
cierra tus ojos y escucha, escucha al mar retumbar
y susurrar, fluir y resonar…*
Me mira medio incrédula
pero hace lo que le digo. Sus ojos se iluminan
cuando oye la magia de la concha. *¡¡Vaya!!*
¡¡El mar está ahí dentro!! - Exclama
regalándome su sonrisa,
la más risueña de las sonrisas.

Flight

To my daughter, Amanda
Soon spring will tremble in your eyes. Mary Ann Mulhern

I am walking slowly
not to shake tomorrow's framework
so I can reach there
because I must – I must and I want to see
my little daughter grow
break out of her chrysalis into her multi-colored flight
of laughter and youth.

I tiptoe onwards
look into the fabric of the future
hide inside its clock
merge with its ticking
and wait *patiently, calmly, hopefully*
as I watch my little one soar towards the light
far from me,
naturally farther every passing second.

I marvel;
and I tremble.

Vuelo

A mi hija, Amanda
Pronto la primavera palpitará en tus ojos. Mary Ann Mulhern

Camino despacio
para no violentar el entramado del mañana
para llegar hasta allá
porque tengo que llegar – tengo y quiero ver
a mi pequeña hija crecer
rasgar su crisálida hacia su vuelo multicolor
de risa y juventud.

Avanzo en puntillas de pie
atisbo en el estambre del futuro
me escondo en su reloj
me fundo a su tictac
y espero *paciente, calmado, esperanzado*
mientras veo a mi pequeña volar en dirección a la luz
lejos de mí,
naturalmente más lejos cada segundo.

Me maravillo;
y me estremezco.

Silent

To my daughter, Amanda
Poetry is… Sandra Phinney
Afraid to speak. Roger Bell
All that's best of dark and bright. George Gordon Byron

I watch you sleep
I convey thoughts and good wishes
silently
let them fly and perch
gently
on your hair.

My words are soundless
for a split eternity
reveling in the harmony
of the dim moonlight
and the shadows
tending sweetly upon you.

I watch
mesmerized
afraid to utter words
and shatter the moment
as you breathe softly in your sleep
unaware
of the silent poetry
I knit for you, my baby,
with pencil and paper.

Callada

A mi hija, Amanda
La poesía es… Sandra Phinney
Sin atreverme a hablar. Roger Bell
Lo mejor de las sombras y las luces. George Gordon Byron

Te miro dormir
transmito pensamientos y buenos deseos
en silencio
los dejo volar y posarse
sigilosamente
en tu pelo.

Mis palabras no suenan
durante una fracción de eternidad
disfrutando la armonía
de la tenue luz de la luna
y las sombras
que convergen tiernamente en ti.

Observo
hipnotizado
sin atreverme a pronunciar palabras
que quiebran el momento
mientras tú respiras suavemente en tu sueño
ajena
a la poesía callada
que tejo para ti, mi niña,
con lápiz y papel.

Plea

To my wife, for Dec. 25, 2008
The feel of you. Milton Acorn
Can we always be this close? Taylor swift

I want to have this more often,
being with you
the warmth of your kiss.

I need
the feel of you always on my flesh
the ever-growing sense of company
to reach the light together
or simply *be* together.

I want this, please,
the overwhelming complexity of life
made simple in your sieve,
darkness
made stars in your irises.

I need all that.

Please tell me
what you need.

Súplica

A mi esposa, por dic. 25, 2008
Sentirte. Milton Acorn
¿Podemos estar siempre así tan cerca? Taylor Swift

Quiero tener esto con más frecuencia,
estar contigo
lo tibio de tu beso.

Necesito
sentirte siempre en mi carne
la sensación siempre creciente de compañía
para alcanzar la luz juntos
o simplemente *estar* juntos.

Quiero esto, por favor,
la complejidad aplastante de la vida
simplificada en tu tamiz,
la oscuridad
trocada en estrellas allí en tus iris.

Necesito todo eso.

Por favor dime
lo que necesitas tú.

Affinities of Pain

To all my friends, who share these affinities of pain...
The loss we carry... Amanda Gorman

These awe-inspiring
affinities of pain hurt us deep
knowing that parting is inevitable. We
never come to terms with death,
the finisher of it all; and we twist
between the illogic sense of our arrival
and the senseless logic of our end
questioning everything
overwhelmed by whys.
These awe-inspiring convergences
native to every living creature—thereat
we flinch when loved ones
cross into eternity
and it is our plight
having to watch them go and
bid them farewell.

Coincidencias del dolor

A todos mis amigos, que comparten estas coincidencias del dolor…
La pérdida que soportamos… Amanda Gorman

Estas sobrecogedoras
coincidencias del dolor nos hieren profundo
al saber que la separación es inevitable. Nosotros
nunca nos adaptamos a la muerte,
la que pone fin a todo; y nos retorcemos
entre el ilógico sentido de nuestra llegada
y la lógica sin sentido de nuestro final
cuestionándolo todo
agobiados por los porqués.
Estas sobrecogedoras convergencias
propias de toda criatura viva—allí
nos estremecemos cuando quienes amamos
cruzan hacia la eternidad
y es nuestra penosa circunstancia
tener que verlos ir y
decirles adiós.

Habit

To my wife, for our moments on the porch
And then the night on a starry hill. Marjorie Pickthall
And we two dreaming the dusk away. Pauline Johnson

Our lasting habit on the porch
our peace-seeking customary rite
of watching the sun's subsiding torch
make way to the shroud of night.

Our gazing into the distant hill
vanishing behind the shadows
our awe, silent and still
as the light of day gradually narrows.

Human witnesses to the afterglows
unique moments, blessed eyes
that see the stars in blazing rows
shine upon us as they rise.

Costumbre

A mi esposa, por nuestros momentos en el balcón
Y entonces la noche sobre una colina estrellada. Marjorie Pickthall
Y nosotros dos soñando todo el crepúsculo. Pauline Johnson

Nuestra duradera costumbre en el portal
nuestro ritual en busca de la paz
observando la antorcha menguante del sol
dar paso al manto de la noche.

Nuestra mirada en la distante colina
que se desvanece detrás de las sombras
nuestro sobrecogimiento, silencioso y sereno
mientras la luz del día se desvanece poco a poco.

Testigos humanos de los anocheceres
momentos únicos, ojos bendecidos
que ven las estrellas en filas resplandecientes
brillar sobre nosotros mientras ascienden.

Becoming Light

... the light from the darkness. Genesis 3:4
... by light and shadow. John B. Lee
... become light. Henry Beissel

I'll take in my hand the darkest
part of night,
stir it gently, add a pinch of stars
until it flickers
like a gem in the raw.
I'll wait for daybreak, then
will hold the gem high
so sun and sky blue polish it
into a brand-new dawn
heir of the cycles of day
with darkness unfailingly
becoming light.

Convirtiéndose en luz

… la luz desde la oscuridad. Génesis 3:4
… en luz y sombra. John B. Lee
… volverse luz. Henry Beissel

Tomaré en mi mano la más oscura
porción de la noche,
la removeré suavemente, agregaré una pizca de estrellas
hasta que resplandezca
como una gema al natural
Esperaré por el alba, entonces
sostendré en alto la gema
para que el sol y el azul del cielo la hagan brillar
hacia un nuevo amanecer
heredero de los ciclos del día
con la oscuridad irrevocablemente
convirtiéndose en luz.

Dawn-gazer

I want to hold this moment. Norma West Linder
At the center of night. James Deahl
... lean on the heart of night. Bliss Carman

5 a.m. face of night
profiled
humid, cold
cricket-pierced

echoes of gypsy cars in the Avenue
silhouettes of early risers
on the street

tall buildings
crack the sky's virginity
still
in the stillness of the hour

street lamps and arms of
antennas
lift the weight of shadows
rotate
towards dawn
s-l-o-w-l-y

a breech in the heart of night
slit bottomless darkness
to bring forth
daybreak

I smile
witness to the cycle,
hold the moment, breathe it in

step from my window

back
to reality.

Espectador del alba

Quiero atrapar este momento. Norma West Linder
Al centro de la noche. James Deahl
… refugiarse en el corazón de la noche. Bliss Carman

La noche con rostro de 5 a.m.
delineado
húmedo, frío
traspasado por los grillos

ecos de carros gitanos en la Avenida
siluetas de gente madrugadora
en la calle

altos edificios
resquebrajan la virginidad del cielo
quietos
en la quietud de la hora

lámparas públicas y brazos de
antenas
levantan el peso de las sombras
rotan
hacia el alba
l-e-n-t-a-m-e-n-t-e

una grieta en el corazón de la noche
infinita oscuridad desgarrada
para entregar
el alba.

Sonrío
testigo de la transición,
atrapo el momento, lo absorbo

me alejo de la ventana

de regreso
a la realidad.

Beyond Sunset

The yellow sky covering itself
with a grey blanket. Katharine Beeman

The day unrolls before my window´s
horizon hungry for a zenith the sun
pursues, conquers
and leaves behind
painting the sky´s span in searing yellow
as it sneaks under a dark blanket
and explodes in a kaleidoscope of dusk colors.
The day endures beyond sunset,
it watches in night disguise awaiting
awaiting, winking star signs at gazers
poets and lovers who
mesmerized by the infinite rotation
of the planets
translate cosmic words
dictated by the moon muses.

Después de la puesta de sol

El cielo amarillo cubriéndose
con una manta gris. Katharine Beeman

El día se esparce ante el horizonte
de mi ventana hambriento de un zenit que el sol
persigue, conquista
y deja atrás
pintando la anchura del cielo en un amarillo intenso
mientras se escabulle bajo un manto oscuro
y explota en un caleidoscopio de colores crepusculares.
El día perdura después de la puesta del sol,
observa con un disfraz nocturno aguardando
aguardando, gesticulando signos de estrellas a espectadores
poetas y amantes quienes
fascinados por la infinita rotación
de los planetas
traducen palabras cósmicas
dictadas por las musas de la luna.

Almighty, Redemptive

... in the presence of light. Henry Beissel

When I pray
light chooses me, a choice I thank
like sunflowers thank their need of sun
and rotate, grateful, thirsty
for illumination. I enter, humbly, the brightness
in full hope it lasts, it endures when
darkness dominates. It will take patience,
confidence, faith to survive,
which I treasure touched by a grace I feel,
I expect haloed by enlightening silence and optimism.
When I pray
I am favored: my prayers are heard more often than not
and things I ask are listened to
because *their* light reaches me
almighty
redemptive.

Todopoderosa, redentora

… en presencia de la luz. Henry Beissel

Cuando oro
la luz me escoge, una elección que agradezco
como los girasoles agradecen su necesidad de sol
y giran, agradecidos, sedientos
de iluminación. Entro, humilde, al resplandor
con total esperanza de que sea duradero, que persista cuando
la oscuridad prevalezca. Tomará paciencia,
confianza, fe para sobrevivir,
lo que atesoro correspondido por una bendición que siento,
espero bajo un halo de edificante silencio y optimismo.
Cuando oro
soy favorecido: mis oraciones son oídas muchas veces
y lo que pido es escuchado
porque *su* luz llega a mí
todopoderosa
redentora.

Lullaby

To my granddaughter, Ahitana

As I watched my beloved daughter
some thirteen years ago,
now I watch my granddaughter cuddle up
when sleepiness is the warmest blanket.
I hate to hear the clock's beep
that'll make her dreams dangle like truncate
leaves and drip oneiric dew. She tosses
and turns, so I become an earthly Hypnos
and quieten her pulse to a whisper
by singing softly and low
nudging sheep to skip over a fence
onto a misty meadow of muffled sounds,
words flowing gently, her mien
of innocence
instilling my own peace.

Canción de cuna

A mi nieta, Ahitana

Igual que miraba a mi querida hija
hace unos trece años,
ahora miro a mi nieta acurrucarse
cuando la soñolencia es la manta más cálida.
Odio escuchar el sonido del reloj
que hará que sus sueños cuelguen como truncas
hojas y goteen rocío onírico. Da vueltas
en la cama, por lo que me convierto en un Hipnos terrenal
y calmo su pulso hasta llevarlo a un susurro
cantándole suave y quedamente
empujando ovejas a saltar una cerca
hasta un prado neblinoso de sonidos apagados,
las palabras fluyendo dulcemente, su semblante
inocente
inspirando mi propia paz.

timely

… with a hunger for sex. Eva Kolacz

you come to the porch
smile a tempting kiss
erotic

our bed two rooms away –
sofa's closer

kids not home…

oportuna

… con hambre de sexo. Eva Kovacz

vienes al portal
sonríes un beso tentador
erótica

nuestro lecho dos habitaciones más allá –
el sofá está más cerca

los chicos no están en casa…

Freedom

Upon the shore beside my wave-lapped feet. Norma West Linder
The lift and lag of an anvil sea. James Deahl
… crystal blue freedom. Ed Woods

elfish winds
awaken sea and sand
again
in my recollections
of dear things

salty aroma
hot grains under
my feet

free-flowing water canvas
tireless ripples
reaching the shoreline
foamy language left behind
after ocean tongues lap
the perennial wetness of the beach

Aeolus sets sails
back and
forth – mighty, prankish:

children's ball abducted
bounced against rock
carried from surf to surf
out
away

whisked off into a deep, blue
freedom…

Libertad

En la orilla junto a mis pies bañados por las olas. Norma West Linder
El ir y venir de un mar de bigornia. James Deahl
… cristalina libertad azul. Ed Woods

vientos juguetones
despiertan mar y arena
otra vez
en mis recuerdos
de cosas queridas

aroma salado
granos calientes bajo
mis pies

lienzo de mar fluyendo libre
ondas incansables
llegan a la orilla
dejan tras de sí un idioma burbujeante
luego que las lenguas del océano besan
la humedad perenne de la playa

Eolo despliega las velas
hacia delante y
hacia atrás – poderoso, travieso:

la pelota de los niños raptada
rebotada contra la roca
llevada de ola en ola
afuera
 lejos

arrastrada hasta una profunda, azul
libertad…

I Listen

Where the waves slap rainbow spray. Norma West Linder
Sea runs to salt beach. James Deahl
Listen to the sea. Laurence Hutchman

my beach awakens
for me
in an ancient wet yawn
carving the rocks
lapping the sleepy sand

then a rumble,
sun cuts through
its glass ripples –

suddenly
sea rainbow flashes
depths brim with life
flow
reveal themselves to me

coral reefs speak in salt language

I listen
in amazement

Escucho

Donde las olas arrojan espuma de arco iris. Norma West Linder
El mar se lanza a la playa salada. James Deahl
Escucha el mar. Laurence Hutchman

mi playa se despierta
para mí
en un antiguo bostezo húmedo
que desgasta las rocas
que besa la soñolienta arena

entonces un fragor,
el sol atraviesa
sus ondas de cristal –

de repente
un arco iris marino relumbra
las profundidades rebosan de vida
fluyen
se revelan a mí

los arrecifes coralinos hablan en idioma de sal

Escucho
asombrado

Enter my Kiss

This warm flesh song. James Deahl
The silver night sent starshine. Norma West Linder
Starlight enters with ancient airs… James Deahl

rain of starlight
streams in
through the window
darkness follows suit; a swan of shadows:

moon's partner
in silver-jet cabrioles
for these wakeful eyes
 of mine

nude silhouette
decorates the bed
unaware
of star ballets, lakes, my eyes –

enter my kiss

A escena mi beso

Esta cálida canción de la carne. James Deahl
La noche plateada envió brillo de estrellas. Norma West Linder
Luz estelar penetra con aires ancestrales... James Deahl

lluvia de luz estelar
irrumpe
por la ventana
le sigue la oscuridad; un cisne de sombras:

pareja de la luna
en cabriolas plateadas-azabaches
para estos insomnes ojos
míos

una silueta desnuda
adorna la cama
sin percatarse
de ballets sidéreos, lagos, mis ojos –

a escena mi beso

Shine

... but shine to be a poem. Richard Grove
... busily write poetry... Kim Grove
Towards the light. Don Gutteridge
... where the fruit hangs... in the heat. Patrick Lane

The sun polishes the trees
with golden shine
warming the fruit to the kernel.

Painting-like highlights of yellow
lure me,
graveled earth feels good beneath my feet
lulled silence embraces.

Poetry is a danseuse, barefoot. Flames
glint in her eyes
while she dances to the rhythm of my quill.

I surrender to her,
 to the shine enveloping me –

these words...

Resplandor

… sino brillar para convertirse en un poema. Richard Grove
… escribir poesía afanosamente… Kim Grove
Hacia la luz. Don Gutteridge
… donde la fruta cuelga… en el calor. Patrick Lane

El sol bruñe los árboles
con un resplandor dorado
calentando la fruta hasta el corazón.

Detalles amarillos como en una pintura
me atraen,
tierra con cascajos sienta bien bajos mis pies
un silencio adormecido abraza.

La poesía es una bailarina, descalza. Llamas
titilan en sus ojos
mientras danza al ritmo de mi pluma.

Me entrego a ella,
al resplandor que me envuelve –

estas palabras…

Your Presence

To the Lord
Give light to my eyes. Psalms 13:3
God gives us Heaven here and now. Bliss Carman
Now I am healing. Bernice Lever

I seek out your presence
Best shelter when I tire.
Beside You my pain lessens
I rest in your warm fire.

I stand under the sun
A man against the years.
With You this humble son –
No worries and no fears.

I pray to You at night
Climb up the darkest slopes
To reach your higher light:
A beacon for my hopes.

Tu presencia

Al Señor
Da luz a mis ojos. Salmos 13:3
Dios nos da el Cielo aquí y ahora. Bliss Carman
Estoy sanando ahora. Bernice Lever

Busco tu presencia
El mejor refugio cuando estoy exhausto.
Contigo mi dolor disminuye
Descanso ante tu tibio fuego.

Me yergo bajo el sol
Un hombre contra los años.
Contigo este humilde hijo –
Sin preocupaciones ni temores.

Oro a ti en las noches
Subo las más oscuras laderas
Para alcanzar tu luz suprema:
Un faro para mis esperanzas.

Today is a moment

To my mother, for Mother´s Day, in memoriam
Honor… thy mother. Deuteronomy 5:16
… to put in words what I feel. Ernesto Galbán

Today is a moment
when my mother comes from eternity
to sit beside me, smile
like the days when she waited for me
gentle in her rocking chair, *"My boy"*
on her lips, arms reaching out
a wave of aromas dancing in the kitchen
with my favorite dishes.
Today is a moment
when she visits my dreams, saves me
from what hurts when life´s darkness
daunts with artful afflictions
with ominous shadows of masks
hanging from the porches. Today
is one of those moments,
and I offer, whole, my affection, my intellect
to pour my best words onto a piece of paper
telling her, before the sacred silence
of her memory, everything
I feel.

May 9th, 2021

Hoy es un momento

A mi madre, por el Día de las Madres, in memóriam
Honrarás… a tu madre. Deuteronomio 5:16
… poner en palabras lo que siento. Ernesto Galbán

Hoy es un momento
en que mi madre viene desde la eternidad
para sentarse a mi lado, sonreír
como los días en que me esperaba
gentil en su balance favorito, *"Mi niño"*
en sus labios, brazos extendidos
ola de aromas danzando en la cocina
con mis platos preferidos.
Hoy es un momento
en que visita mis sueños, me salva
de lo que hiere cuando lo oscuro de la vida
intimida con males arteros
con sombras ominosas de máscaras
colgando en los portales. Hoy
es uno de esos momentos,
y entrego, enteros, mi afecto, mi intelecto
para poner mis mejores palabras en un papel
diciéndole, ante el solemne silencio
de su recuerdo, todo
lo que siento.

Mayo 9, 2021

dancer's name

The dancer... beautiful throat... Hugh Hazelton
For me you are both the dancer and the dance. Don Gutteridge
A girl dances for me. Belkis Mendez

dancer without a name on TV
light ebony shining
full length
rapids of curly hair flowing towards infinity
her voice jingles out of the screen
mulatto drums in her laughter
sway of hips defies the physics of the universe

dancer without a name
transcends the TV show
fleeting seconds
a dance with Eros

Africa is her name

el nombre de la bailarina

La bailarina… Hermosa garganta. Hugh Hazelton
Para mí eres ambas, bailarina y baile. Don Gutteridge
Una chica baila para mí. Belkis Mendez

bailarina sin nombre en la televisión
ébano claro reluciendo
de cuerpo entero
rápidos de pelo encrespado fluyendo al infinito
su voz tintinea más allá de la pantalla
tambores mulatos en su risa
el movimiento de caderas desafía la física del universo

bailarina sin nombre
trasciende el espectáculo televisivo
segundos vertiginosos
un baile con Eros

África es su nombre

Shapes

To my daughter, Amanda
(Remember when we looked at the clouds together?)
... the clouds that streak their layer to the horizon. Allan Briesmaster
... the shifting... clouds that I envisioned. Andreas Gripp

kodak afternoon sky
its frontier line propped by
rolling cordillera
proud ships of clouds
adrift in the skymap
prows pointed upwards/downwards
towards a beyond
cotton floats perhaps
pageant of white sugar
rightwards, a long
mystic horned fish preying on the city
fluffed streaks
like sitting lions
tents, gliding birds, butterflies
– infinite shapes –

tired clouds
rest on a host hill
fish become snakes, lions are balls now
floats are dinosaurs, ships are grey-silvery lines...

they moisten a crowd of trees and shrubs
beneath them
ceiba, cedar, eucalyptus, pines, coffee,
in return, flowers tickle the clouds

shape-changing, incessant, haphazard
metamorphoses
often, sadly
unnoticed to us

Formas

A mi hija, Amanda
(¿Recuerdas cuando mirábamos las nubes juntos?)
… las nubes que echan su manto sobre el horizonte. Allan Briesmaster
… el paso… de las nubes que yo imaginaba. Andreas Gripp

memorable cielo vespertino
su línea fronteriza apuntalada por
una ondulante cordillera
orgullosos veleros de nubes
a la deriva en el mapa del cielo
proas apuntando arriba/abajo
hacia un más allá
carrozas de algodón tal vez
un desfile de blanca azúcar
a la derecha, un largo
místico pez con cornamenta acechando la ciudad
bandas esponjosas
como leones echados
tiendas de campaña, aves planeando, mariposas
– formas infinitas –

nubes cansadas
descansan sobre una colina anfitriona
los peces se vuelven serpientes, los leones son pelotas ahora
las carrozas son dinosaurios, los veleros son líneas gris-plateadas…

humedecen una multitud de árboles y arbustos
debajo de ellas
ceiba, cedro, eucalipto, pinos, café
en pago, reciben el cosquilleo de las flores

formas cambiantes, indetenibles, casuales
metamorfosis
frecuentemente, tristemente
inadvertidas por nosotros

Fortune

I'd never learn to dance with any other girl. Robert Currie

Upon you tend the loftiness of the sea
and the inexhaustible thrust of salt and water
breaking against me, the vulnerable shore,

expansive, wet, eager
to clash with your seafaring bubbles.

Upon us tends the elliptical trajectory
of the planets aligning auspiciously
to build a shelter for you and me
to leave an imprint of two people
amidst black holes
and nascent stars.

We dance with the universe, fortune
of a few: you and I
the chosen ones.

Suerte

Nunca aprendería a bailar con ninguna otra chica. Robert Currie

Hacia ti tienden la grandeza del mar
y el empuje infinito de sal y agua
rompiendo sobre mí, la orilla vulnerable,

vasta, húmeda, ansiosa
por chocar con tus espumas marinas.

Hacia nosotros tiende la trayectoria elíptica
de los planetas que se alinean propiciamente
para formar un refugio para ti y para mí
dejar una huella de dos personas
entre orificios negros
y estrellas nacientes.

Bailamos con el universo, suerte
de unos pocos: tú y yo
los escogidos.

Daybreak

… between darkness and light. Joseph A. Farina

The night tucks itself into
cozy rooftops
twinkling stars bat their eyelashes
to lull the city.

From my porch I listen to
hours become,
grow, and perish
after giving birth to baby hours
wound inside a nonstop timefulness.

The nightscape yawns
windmills of silence wheel into
tomorrow —

The new day discovers me
envelops my dreams with a dewy blanket
and breaks into colors and sounds

without waking me up.

Amanecer

... entre la oscuridad y la luz. Joseph A. Farina

La noche se acomoda en
confortables azoteas
astros titilantes mueven sus pestañas
para adormecer la ciudad.

Desde mi balcón escucho
las horas ser,
crecer, y morir
después de dar a luz a horas-bebés
devanadas dentro de una imparable temporalidad

El paisaje nocturno bosteza
molinos de silencio ruedan hacia
el mañana –

El nuevo día me descubre
envuelve mis sueños en un manto de rocío
e irrumpe en colores y sonidos

sin despertarme.

Memories

To my 84-year-old father,
for Father's Day, June 20th, 2021
Honor thy father. Deuteronomy 5:16

It hurts to see your spirit cave in
under the burden of Time, unforgiving years
collecting on your shoulders like blankets of age,
heavily cold, coldly heavy. It was me, long ago, on those
shoulders. I remember. I was a merry jockey up there,
my rein your thinning hair or your ears,
me barefoot with my make-believe spurs prodding your chest
so you´d carry me around, so you´d take your
fond-of-horses son out to the street to rival coaches.
I remember. Now, I carry you. Less jollity, more pain
lancing down your legs. *I´m far too old*, you complain,
looking me in the eye as if asking for an explanation.
I cringe at the inevitability of tomorrow—or yesterday,
when eternity stole Mom away. I remember.
Can hardly walk, you mumble. The joyous trots of past days
have cantered down to an effortful walker-assisted shuffle
trying to beat the distance between your bed
and the nearby rocking chair that seems to be, in your mind,
a million miles away. You used to bike to and
from work. I remember. You used to race fishes
in the beach, run athlete-like, carry Mom in your arms…
Today, those memories vanish for you but not for me:
I was there with you, you guided me, you prompted me,
you taught me. I rekindle those stories, retell them
to cheer you up. You say *Thank you*, faintly giving me
a smile of gratitude I´ll always remember.

Recuerdos

A mi padre de 84 años,
por el Día de los Padres, Junio 20, 2021
Honrarás a tu padre. Deuteronomio 5:16

Duele ver tu espíritu ceder
bajo la carga del Tiempo, años implacables
que se amontonan sobre tus hombros como mantas de edad,
pesadamente frías, fríamente pesadas. Era yo, hace mucho, sobre esos
hombros. Recuerdo. Yo era un dichoso jinete allá arriba,
mi rienda tu pelo escaso o tus orejas,
yo descalzo con mis espuelas de fantasía hincando tu pecho
para que me llevaras de paseo, para que llevaras a tu
hijo aficionado a los caballos hasta la calle para competir con los carruajes.
Recuerdo. Ahora, te cargo yo. Menos júbilo, más dolor
clavándose por tus piernas. *Estoy demasiado viejo*, te quejas,
mirándome a los ojos como si pidieras una explicación.
Me encojo ante la inevitabilidad del mañana—o del ayer,
cuando la eternidad nos robó a Mamá. Recuerdo.
Casi no puedo caminar, murmuras. Los alegres trotes de días pasados
han decaído a un esforzado arrastre de pies ayudado por el andador
intentando vencer la distancia entre tu cama
y el cercano balance que parece estar, en tu mente,
a un millón de millas de distancia. Solías ir en bicicleta hasta y
de regreso de tu trabajo. Recuerdo. Solías rivalizar con los peces
en la playa, correr como un atleta, llevar a Mamá en tus brazos…
Hoy, esos recuerdos se desvanecen en ti pero no en mí:
yo estaba allí contigo, tú me guiaste, tú me motivaste,
tú me enseñaste. Revivo esas historias, las digo de nuevo
para animarte. Me dices *Gracias*, débilmente sonriéndome
con una gratitud que siempre recordaré.

falter for an instant

My soul is weary of my life. Job 10:1
We walk in blindness and dark night
Through half our earthly way;
Our clouds of weaknesses obscure
The glory of the day. Charles Sangster

my head is spinning today
and I sit on the edge of everything
to regain balance, to ponder
to self-complain—a relief valve—in this corner
I´ve tumbled to, mumbling disgruntled thoughts
that weigh heavily, won´t let me breathe
the way a soul should breathe

                          my eyes are over-flooded
and I shut them off from everything
to seek inside what cannot be found
out there in the maelstrom of a life
that looms large and baffling
over our weary heads
and presses down hard. I falter for an instant
yet try to shake it all off
with fortitude, faith and prayer to see me through
at least two and a half more decades.

dudar por un momento

Mi alma está desalentada de mi vida. Job 10:1
Caminamos a ciegas y en noche lóbrega
La mitad de nuestra ruta terrenal;
Nuestras nubes de debilidad oscurecen
La gloria del día. Charles Sangster

mi cabeza da vueltas hoy
y me siento al borde de todo
para recuperar mi equilibrio, para meditar
para auto-quejarme—una válvula de escape—en esta esquina
a la que he venido a dar, mascullando pensamientos de insatisfacción
que pesan excesivamente, no me dejan respirar
de la forma en que un alma debe respirar

                              mis ojos están más que anegados
y los aíslo de todo
para buscar dentro lo que no se puede hallar
allá afuera en el torbellino de una vida
que amenaza y desconcierta
nuestras agotadas cabezas
y presiona fuertemente. Dudo por un momento
pero intento superarlo todo
con fortaleza, fe y plegaria para que me ayuden
al menos dos décadas y media más.

Cycles of Life

To Jorge Pérez and Manuel Velázquez, in our shared losses...

When our parents
are laid to rest in their final place
a curtain falls, a painful divide opens
between our past and us. Somehow
the thread that keeps us connected to childhood days
loosens, yesterday is blurred,
full colors and joys are dimmed as an awkwardness
of helplessness and nonsense
unsettles our hearts, never to leave.
When our parents go
a part inside us follows them in an attempt
to defy death, rescue our roots
watch over them as they watched over us,
while the other part necessarily heads towards
tomorrow holding on to our beloved ones, those who
across the endless cycles of life
will safeguard too their memories of us.

Los ciclos de la vida

A Jorge Pérez y Manuel Velázquez, por nuestras pérdidas compartidas…

Cuando nuestros padres
son llevados a su último lugar de reposo
cae una cortina, se abre un doloroso abismo
entre nuestro pasado y nosotros. De alguna forma
el hilo que nos mantiene unidos a nuestra niñez
cede, el ayer se enturbia,
los colores plenos y las alegrías disminuyen mientras una desazón
de vulnerabilidad y sin sentido
disturba nuestros corazones, para nunca irse.
Cuando nuestros padres se marchan
parte de nosotros los sigue intentando
desafiar la muerte, rescatar nuestras raíces
protegerlos como ellos nos protegieron a nosotros,
mientras la otra parte se encamina necesariamente hacia
el mañana aferrada a nuestros seres queridos, aquellos que
a lo largo de los infinitos ciclos de la vida
guardarán también sus recuerdos de nosotros.

Awe

... when the sun dips... under the wave. Susan Ioannou

I've seen the evening dip its darkness
in the sea
slowly embrace the waves.
I've seen it turn cold and vast.

I've felt their united might
swallow time and space

and I've been overwhelmed by their greatness,
awed deep in my heart.

Sobrecogimiento

… cuando el sol se hunde… bajo la ola. Susan Ioannou

He visto al anochecer hundir su oscuridad
en el mar
abrazar lentamente las olas.
Lo he visto volverse frío e inmenso.

He sentido sus poderes juntos
devorar el tiempo y el espacio

y he quedado abrumado por su grandeza,
sobrecogido profundamente en mi corazón.

Moment

… a single, glistening instant. James Deahl
… where the soul and the spirit meet and float. John B. Lee

Think of this moment as our power
to cross the skein of time
suspend it right here
right now.
We escape its tyranny
dive deep into each other's skin
– a rediscovery of sighs, cues, desires –
and we smile, eyes half-closed
purring like felines
at the peak of their estrus.

Think of this instant as our magic
to transcend
travel into ourselves, stamp
our signatures
on our souls,

hold eternity in our ultimate cry
and be on the verge of faint
clinging to chunks of breathless words,

closeness of the lips and hands translating
into this poem
what we feel.

Momento

... un exclusivo, esplendoroso instante. James Deahl
... donde el alma y el espíritu se encuentran y emergen. John B. Lee

Piensa que este momento es nuestro poder
para cruzar la madeja del tiempo
detenerlo aquí mismo
ahora mismo.
Escapamos de su tiranía
nos sumergimos profundo en nuestras pieles
– un redescubrir suspiros, señales, deseos –
y sonreímos, ojos entornados
ronroneando como felinos
en el zenit de su estro.

Piensa que este instante es nuestro sortilegio
para trascender
viajar hacia nosotros, plasmar
nuestras firmas
sobre nuestras almas,

alcanzar la eternidad en nuestro grito final
y estar a punto de desmayarnos
aferrados a trozos de palabras jadeantes,

la cercanía de labios y manos expresando
en este poema
lo que sentimos.

muse interruptus – call

Fluttering nude calling me... Ernesto Galbán
She reaches out to him. Norma West Linder
You interrupt my poem. Tracey Gunne

ridge of jagged hills
blunt/sharp
against the horizon

it punctures the skyline
that bleeds cotton lining
rolling nonstop so far-off
my eyes
 hurt and blink

I scribble away a bit more of
up
and
down
poetry
until
you groan
next to me

nude skin calling…

musa interrumpida – llamado

Un desnudo palpitante llamándome... Ernesto Galbán
Ella se le acerca. Norma West Linder
Interrumpes mi poema. Tracey Gunne

cordillera de lomas irregulares
 despuntadas/puntiagudas
en el horizonte

perfora la línea del cielo
que sangra un tapiz de algodón
ondulando sin parar tan lejos
que mis ojos
me duelen y parpadean

sigo escribiendo un poco más de
poesía
de
altos
y
bajos
hasta que
gimes
a mi lado

piel desnuda llamándome...

muse interruptus – shower

One glimpse, one wink. Marion Mutala
Reaching out now for your touch. Denis Robillard

I've been watching it
trying to capture it in my lines,

imposing cumulonimbus
low-lying, somber
eager to shed thick tears. Pricked by
clipped hill rims
it showers the fields, profusely

you've been watching too
patiently purring in bed. Your eyelashes
wink –

I pause in my poetic pursuit and reach out

to be cleansed in your nude version of rain

musa interrumpida – lluvia

Una mirada, un guiño. Marion Mutala
Acercándome ahora para que me toques. Denis Robillard

lo he estado mirando
intentando plasmarlo en mis líneas,

cumulonimbo imponente
bajo, sombrío
ansioso por derramar gruesas lágrimas. Punzado por
los entrecortados filos de la colina
se vierte sobre los campos, profusamente

tú has estando mirando también
ronroneando pacientemente en cama. Tus pestañas
hacen un guiño –

hago una pausa en mi búsqueda poética y me acerco

para ser purificado en tu versión desnuda de la lluvia

Somewhere

Hot hand slides pressing on veins, on muscles. James Deahl
Moon waxed golden when we loved. Norma West Linder
What riotous emotions she is unleashing. Bernice Lever

she holds seeds of pleasure
in her hands
scatters them on my skin
gently
softly humming
so they grow
cosmic towards a sun
somewhere in her galaxy

she keeps geisha secrets
in her eyes
spills them in my ears
sweetly
groaning playfully
so I spin
faithful into her orbit
somewhere in her anatomy

she bleeds desires honed
in her lips
shoots them into my arteries
eagerly
unbridled, surrendering/commanding
so I live and die
willingly under her spell
somewhere between my years
of ended innocence
and my grave

En algún lugar

Mano ardiente se mueve presionando venas, músculos. James Deahl
La luna se tornó dorada cuando nos amamos. Norma West Linder
Qué desenfrenadas emociones desata ella. Bernice Lever

lleva semillas de placer
en sus manos
las esparce sobre mi piel
gentilmente
tarareando plácidamente
para que crezcan
cósmicas hacia un sol
en algún lugar de su galaxia

guarda secretos de geisha
en sus ojos
los revela en mis oídos
dulcemente
gimiendo traviesa
para que yo gire
fiel hacia su órbita
en algún lugar de su anatomía

sangra deseos afilados
en sus labios
los lanza por mis arterias
impacientemente
desbocada, entregada/dominante
para que yo viva y muera
voluntariamente bajo su hechizo
en algún lugar entre mis años
de inocencia perdida
y mi sepulcro

Rendezvous

I belong to my lover, and his desire is for me. Song of Songs 7:10
I remember the moist warmth of your flesh. James Deahl
... live for your body like a soul possessed
reside within the incredible dominion of your flesh. John B. Lee

There´s a taste lingering
gentle and evocative
when we must end this night
and the pleasures sparked
in our bodies´ intimate awareness.
It resists fading
deep where feelings pulse
and under the skin we remember
the proud remnants
of the hours that refuse to bid farewell
to a handsome full moon.
Harmony danced
out of our bonded breaths
yet we must part
to face life out there
to lose ourselves in routines
smiling once in a while
as we savor our rendezvous
quietly, wistfully
and recall the sensation
that fondles the lips
that nips the mind.
There´s a persisting hint
in flesh and psyche:
experience´s embers aglow
reminiscent, rekindling
until desire cannot withhold us any more
and brings us back together
so we unite
our bodies again
and rewrite the meanings of rapture
in yet another rendezvous.

Cita

Soy de mi amado, y su deseo es por mí. Cantar de los Cantares 7:10
Recuerdo la húmeda calidez de tu piel. James Deahl
… vivir para tu cuerpo como un alma poseída
residir dentro del increíble dominio de tu carne. John B. Lee

Hay un gusto que permanece
plácido y evocativo
cuando tenemos que finalizar esta noche
y los placeres desatados
en el íntimo conocimiento de nuestros cuerpos.
Resiste esfumarse
profundo donde los sentimientos palpitan
y bajo la piel recordamos
los orgullosos vestigios
de las horas que se niegan a decir adiós
a una apuesta luna llena.
La armonía danzó
desde nuestros acoplados alientos
pero debemos irnos
a afrontar la vida allá afuera
perdernos en las rutinas
sonriendo de vez en cuando
mientras saboreamos nuestra cita
calladamente, nostálgicamente
y rememoramos la sensación
que acaricia los labios
que mordisquea la mente.
Hay una insinuación persistente
en la carne y la psiquis:
brasas encendidas de lo experimentado
sugerentes, reavivantes
hasta que el deseo no nos puede detener más
y nos junta otra vez
para que unamos
nuestros cuerpos nuevamente
y reescribamos los significados del éxtasis
en otra cita más.

she wakes up

Let's have dreams blooming. Eva Kolacz

sudden wind blows in
bed sheet glides
and
falls

bold air dabs sweat
from her nudity;

dreams start to ripen:
she wakes up – sleepy fruit –
to my caress

ella despierta

Tengamos sueños que florezcan. Eva Kolacz

viento repentino sopla
la sábana se desliza
y
cae

el aire atrevido seca suavemente el sudor
de su desnudez;

los sueños comienzan a madurar:
ella despierta – fruta adormilada –
a mi caricia

wings of desire

… your whole self taken away. Lynda Monahan
… you… the worshipper… of my desire. Eva Kolacz
I caress her wings. Robert Sward

hot night
warm bed
no need for her to wear a nightie

all she has on
are wings of desire
we fly…

alas de deseo

… todo tu ser raptado. Lynda Monahan
… tú… el idólatra… de mi deseo. Eva Kolacz
Acaricio sus alas. Robert Sward

noche calurosa
lecho tibio
no necesita usar camisola

todo lo que tiene puesto
son alas de deseo
volamos…

11 non-Haiku / 11 no-Haikus

1

Every sunset / Each unique. Sarah Richardson

evening rounds
sun dives in skyline
sizzling dusk

1

Cada puesta del sol / Cada una única. Sarah Richardson

ciclos nocturnos
el sol se hunde en el horizonte
crepúsculo crepitante

2

The first bare trees. James Deahl

fall glides in
baring crowns of trees:
leaf stealer

2

Los primeros árboles desnudos. James Deahl

el otoño llega
desnudando las copas de los árboles:
ladrón de hojas

3

huge night screen
hanging from jet sky –
shooting star

3

inmensa pantalla de la noche
colgando del cielo azabache –
estrella fugaz

4

The evening star goes to bed… John Hamley

night bed made
stars doze off in blinks
moon yawning

4

La estrella vespertina se va a la cama… John Hamley

lecho nocturno listo
las estrellas se quedan dormidas en parpadeos
la luna bosteza

5

feller moon
axes the tree bough
it bleeds light

5

luna leñadora
corta la rama del árbol
que sangra luz

6

... the moon shining over... Laurence Hutchman

Clock stutters.
Through lit window, moon
winds it up.

6

... la luna iluminando... Laurence Hutchman

El reloj tartamudea.
A través de la alumbrada ventana, la luna
le da cuerda.

7

The moment: a still photo. Donna Allard
Birds in soft flight. Sarah Richardson

birds dot clouds
flap wings towards sky –
a snapshot

7

El momento: una foto inmóvil. Donna Allard
Aves en suave vuelo. Sarah Richardson

aves puntean las nubes
baten alas hacia el cielo –
una foto

8

How God sees. Susan McMaster

Gold beacon
beaming through the trees.
God's glory.

8

Como Dios ve. Susan McMaster

Faro de oro
resplandeciendo entre los árboles.
La gloria de Dios.

9

… the whisper of water… Eva Kolacz

sea kissing
shore groaning softly…
they make love

9

… el murmullo del agua… Eva Kolacz

el mar besando
la orilla gimiendo suavemente…
hacen el amor

10

… a shaft of sun. Jan Wood

dog´s bark cracks
the mirror of dawn;
sun mends it

10

… un rayo de sol. Jan Wood

un ladrido de perro quiebra
el espejo del alba;
el sol lo repara

11

… singing kisses. Elana Wolff

tree bough leans
onto crooning stream:
rippled kiss

11

… besos cantores… Elana Wolff

la rama del árbol se inclina
sobre el arroyo cantor:
beso ondulado

Continuity

To my parents, Zenaida Iglesias (the "Galician") and Miguel Olivé
... immortalizing the memories. Don Gutteridge

I have a connection with rocking chairs,
both dad and mom loved their wooden ones
and ended the day comfortably seated before our ancient
black-and-white, light-bulb, two-channel TV set.
Almost fifty years later that image stays with me,
it recurred when I came from school weekends
and entered the cement pathway leading to my door:
I instantly saw my mother smiling from her rocker
a gift of guava pies baking in the oven, black bean soup
boiling in the pressure cooker and *ensalada fría* reaching *
my nose, awakening my taste buds. She knew how I craved
her cooking after a week away from home...
When I visit my childhood house – not ours any more –
I am blessed again with those visions and memories strong
enough to endure. There are reminders of those years here now
with my eighty-four-year-old father who takes toddler steps
out to the patio where his favorite rocking chair, today
a rubber one, awaits for him to sunbathe, and continuity is
safe in seeing my daughters and granddaughter rock their
happiness in their own rockers watching cartoons
in their flat-screen, multi-channel, color TV.

* *Poet's note: Ensalada fría: A chicken-and-pineapple-based salad enhanced with boiled potato dice (my mother never used spaghetti,noodles, macaroni or ravioli of any kind), dressed with home-made mayonnaise (she had her own recipe for this too) and decorated on the surface with slices of sweet pepper. Mom would not let my sister or me touch it until it had cooled in the fridge for a few hours. It was heaven in food form.*

Continuidad

A mis padres, Zenaida Iglesias (la "Gallega") y Miguel Olivé
… inmortalizando los recuerdos. Don Gutteridge

Tengo una conexión con los balances,
tanto mi papá como mi mamá adoraban los suyos de madera
y terminaban el día sentados cómodamente frente a nuestro vetusto
televisor en blanco y negro, de bombillas, de dos canales.
Casi cincuenta años después esa imagen permanece conmigo,
se repetía cuando yo llegaba de la escuela los fines de semana
y entraba al camino de cemento que llevaba a mi puerta:
enseguida veía a mi madre sonriendo desde su balance
un regalo de pasteles de guayaba horneándose, potaje de frijoles negros
hirviendo en la olla de presión y *ensalada fría* alcanzando *
mi nariz, despertando mis papilas gustativas. Ella sabía cuánto yo anhelaba
su comida después de una semana lejos de casa…
Cuando visito mi casa de la niñez – ya no es nuestra –
soy bendecido otra vez con esas visiones y recuerdos lo suficientemente
fuertes para perdurar. Hay recordatorios de esos años aquí ahora
con mi padre de ochenta y cuatro años que da pasos de niño pequeño
hasta el patio donde su balance preferido, hoy
de goma, lo espera para que tome sol, y la continuidad está
segura al ver a mis hijas y mi nieta mecer su
felicidad en sus propios balances mirando muñequitos
en su televisor de pantalla plana, de muchos canales, a color.

* Nota del poeta: Ensalada fría: una ensalada a base de pollo y piña mejorada con trozos hervidos
de papa (mi madre nunca usó espaguetis, fideos, macarrones o ravioles de ningún tipo),
aderezada con mayonesa casera (ella tenía su propia receta para esto también, y
decorada en la superficie con tajadas de pimienta dulce. Mamá no nos permitía ni a mi
hermana ni a mí tocar la ensalada hasta tanto se hubiera refrescado en el
refrigerador por unas horas. Era el cielo en forma de comida.

This Poem

I am thankful when the muses visit. John B. Lee
Beyond that, and more importantly; this is poetry. Manuel Velázquez

The afternoon snoozes placidly next to me,
around me. Green-golden still life that is anything but
still drifts about as a balmy wind sings
in the drowsy tree branches,
echoes of distant cars defy distance,
a polychrome butterfly communes with the garden
and restless birds chirp away refusing to take a nap.
The afternoon yawns filling the hour with falling leaves
intermittent bits of lulling peace plus a plethora of sunlight
cascading onto the buildings. I find shade and quiet
to translate images before my eyes,
emotions tickling my skin
thoughts whirling into words swimming
back and forth the air that surrounds me voiced by
wooing muses, and in the wooing
this poem.

Este poema

Agradezco cuando las musas me visitan. John B. Lee
Además, y sobre todo; esto es poesía. Manuel Velázquez

La tarde dormita apaciblemente cerca de mí,
a mi alrededor. Verde-dorada naturaleza muerta que es todo menos
muerta se desplaza mientras un adormecedor viento canta
en las aletargadas ramas de los árboles,
ecos de distantes carros retan la distancia,
una mariposa policromada conversa íntimamente con el jardín
y aves inquietas gorjean negándose a echar una siesta.
La tarde bosteza colmando la hora con hojas que caen
ratos intermitentes de aquietante paz más un raudal de luz solar
cayendo sobre los edificios. Encuentro sombra y sosiego
para traducir las imágenes ante mis ojos,
las emociones cosquilleando mi piel
los pensamientos haciéndose palabras que atraviesan
en ida y vuelta el aire que me rodea articuladas por
musas arrulladoras, y en el arrullo
este poema.

Lunch

Wishing that gulls… John Hamley
Nature… holds stories woven and infinite.
Sarah Richardson
… searching for my dinner in the large
restaurant of the sea. Laurence Hutchman

A seagull scans
the ocean menu
bird's eye view first
then low-flying reconnaissance
wings spread
beak ready
lining the rippled diamond
far from where humans
swim   splash   scare
fish away.

She targets a *plat du jour*
plummets
beak clamps something
resurfaces –
contortionist fish,
                             lunch.

Almuerzo

Deseando que las gaviotas... John Hamley
La naturaleza… tiene historias urdidas e infinitas.
Sarah Richardson
… buscando mi comida en el gran restaurante del
mar. Laurence Hutchman

Una gaviota explora
el menú del océano
vista panorámica primero
luego rastreo a baja altura
alas desplegadas
pico listo
dejando una raya en el ondulado diamante
lejos de donde los humanos
nadan   chapotean   asustan
a los peces.

Apunta a un *especial del día*
se lanza en picada
el pico sujeta algo
vuelve a la superficie –
pez contorsionista,
                              almuerzo

Burial Day

On my mother's demise (January 18th, 2005)
... your smile's... embrace has always rescued me. Richard Grove

Silence, silence
of farewell and tear,
the graveyard... the loss
so searing, so near.
Silence, silence
overwhelming and loud,
a coffin conceals her
our faces all bowed.
Silence, silence
floats densely in the air,
a tombstone with her name
too hefty to bear.
Silence, silence
no rescue? no hope?
the gate locks her up –
God, teach us to cope.

Día de funeral

En el fallecimiento de mi madre (Enero 18, 2005)
  … el abrazo… de tu sonrisa me ha salvado siempre. Richard Grove

Silencio, silencio
de adiós y de lágrima,
el sepulcro… la pérdida
tan abrasadora, tan cercana.
Silencio, silencio
abrumador y estridente,
un ataúd la oculta
nuestros rostros inclinados.
Silencio, silencio
que flota denso en el aire,
una lápida con su nombre
demasiado pesada para soportarla.
Silencio, silencio
¿no hay salvación? ¿no hay esperanza?
la verja la encierra –
Dios, enséñanos a resistir.

New Work Day

I'll live to work another day. James Deahl

I watch the day light up
from silence and shadows
to noise and clarity.

People emerge from their homes
repopulate sidewalks and streets
fill the foggy outdoor world,
some idle with clatter and clutter
some hurry with discretion and diligence.

I must join the rhythm of life
so set the coffee cup on the porch table
lift myself up from my cozy armchair
and climb down the sleepy stairs
to merge – discreet and diligent –
with the rolling crowd

into a new work day.

Nuevo día de trabajo

Viviré para trabajar otro día. James Deahl

Observo el día iluminarse
del silencio y las sombras
al ruido y la claridad.

La gente sale de sus hogares
repueblan aceras y calles
llenan el brumoso mundo exterior,
algunos holgazanean en estrépito y desorden
algunos se apuran con discreción y diligencia.

Debo unirme al ritmo de la vida
por eso pongo mi taza de café sobre la mesa del balcón
me levanto de mi cómodo sillón
y bajo las soñolientas escaleras
para mezclarme – discreto y diligente –
con la multitud ondulante

hacia un nuevo día de trabajo.

To Face the Day

… the beautiful life of the day. John B. Lee
… into today. Norma West Linder
Eyes open to the new dawn. Fran Figge

Peaceful candor floats
early in the morning
over the Holguín valley.

Waves of expanding blue
ignite the city
hill outcrops tint
a far-away of clouds
from where a sun strolls up proud and imposing.

Dawn canopies the world in seconds
a host of sounds and sights proclaim it:
strings of lives
dots in motion
emerging from the realm of darkness
into the light –

Shifting from sleep into consciousness
tossing and turning in bed,
I awake
to face the day.

Para enfrentar el día

... la primorosa vida del día. John B. Lee
... hacia el día. Norma West Linder
Los ojos se abren al nuevo amanecer. Fran Figge

Una serena bondad flota
temprano en la mañana
sobre el valle de Holguín.

Olas de azul se difunden
ponen en marcha la ciudad
afloramientos de colinas colorean
una distancia de nubes
desde donde sale a pasear un sol orgulloso e imponente.

El alba cubre el mundo en segundos
una multitud de sonidos y visiones la anuncian:
sucesiones de vidas
puntos en movimiento
alejándose del reino de la oscuridad
rumbo a la luz —

Pasando del sueño a la vigilia
dando vueltas en la cama,
me despierto
para enfrentar el día.

this image

In collaboration with Antony Di Nardo
... the divinity of blue. Richard Grove

cotton shapes
an azure mantle, this accord
of white and blue:

under infinity antennas sigh and aim at
perfect heights

this image

holds a pen
unfolds a sheet, perpetuates

words

esta imagen

En colaboración con Antony Di Nardo
… lo divino del azul. Richard Grove

figuras de algodón
manto de añil, esta armonía
de blanco y azul:

bajo lo infinito las antenas suspiran y apuntan hacia
alturas perfectas

esta imagen

toma una pluma
abre una hoja de papel, perpetúa

palabras

Of Your Seasons

To my wife, worried about age…
There's beauty in the change of seasons. Patrick Connors

Seasons visit you, quietly. Flowers
you have planted bloom and eventually fade
with the cycles;
but you are always blossoming.

Winter has generously frozen
time
in your flesh.

Spring becomes you. Wilted flowers
tremble back to life
murmuring about pollen and sunlight
as you spread your wings
and take flight merging with a rainbow.

Summer brings tides of heat,
it comes nude, like you
tiptoeing out of the shower
into our bedroom, allowing me a peek
at your eternity.

Autumn comes, silently. Dry leaves
dance onto the soil that welcomes them.
It is your feast now: You let
your towel fall
from your hand,
like leaves…

… I kneel to pick it up
and you make me
Knight of your seasons.

De tus estaciones

A mi esposa, preocupada por la edad…
Hay belleza en el ciclo de las estaciones. Patrick Connors

Las estaciones llegan hasta ti, dulcemente. Las flores
que has sembrado dan frutos y eventualmente se marchitan
con los ciclos;
pero tú siempre estás floreciendo.

El invierno ha detenido generosamente
el tiempo
en tu carne.

La primavera te asienta. Las flores marchitas
se estremecen de vuelta a la vida
murmurando sobre polen y luz de sol
mientras abres tus alas
y alzas el vuelo fundiéndote con un arco iris.

El verano trae mareas de calor,
anda desnudo, como tú
saliendo de la ducha
en puntillas hasta nuestro cuarto, permitiéndome descubrir
tu eternidad.

Llega el otoño, en silencio. Hojas secas
danzan hasta el suelo que les da la bienvenida.
Es tu convite ahora: Dejas
caer la toalla
de tu mano,
como las hojas…

… me arrodillo para recogerla
y me nombras
Caballero de tus estaciones.

Silent Night

Silent night. Nat King Cole
Mysterious night. Joseph Blanco White
After the afterglow. Denis Robillard

Silent night settles shyly
upon the city.
It hovers between hesitation and resolution
takes possession of my porch
one warm floor tile to the next
trying to seal my lips
to quiet the onrush of eager words
about to be spilt into the air;

but it cannot restrain my hand
which speaks for me in
multi-shape calligraphies of my feelings
molding them into vibrations of the heart
that turn this silent night into

a mysterious string of poems.

Noche silenciosa

Noche silenciosa. Nat King Cole
Noche misteriosa. Joseph Blanco White
Después del crepúsculo. Denis Robillard

La noche silenciosa se posa tímida
sobre la ciudad.
Flota entre la duda y la determinación
se adueña de mi balcón
una tibia baldosa tras otra
tratando de sellar mis labios
calmar la ola de palabras impacientes
a punto de ser lanzadas al aire;

pero no puede retener mi mano
que habla por mí en
múltiples caligrafías de mis sentimientos
moldeándolos en vibraciones del corazón
que convierten esta noche silenciosa en

una misteriosa sucesión de poemas.

Writing

... and our immortality. Bernice Lever
... the soul that moves the hand. John B. Lee
... of craft and word. Ruth Latta

The sounds of silence
speak to poets
translating signs and semantics
that blend into word-rhythms
showering stardust letters
onto the still sheets of paper.

The sounds of silence visit.
Above apparent muteness
ride the Muses of Poetry
deep-spurring the flanks of creation

weeping
giving birth
to the never-ending craft of writing.

Escribir

... y nuestra inmortalidad. Bernice Lever
... el espíritu que estremece la mano. John B. Lee
... del arte y la palabra. Ruth Latta

Los sonidos del silencio
les hablan a los poetas
traduciendo signos y semántica
que se mezclan en palabras-ritmos
derramando letras de polvo estelar
sobre las inmóviles hojas de papel.

Los sonidos del silencio visitan.
Sobre su aparente mutismo
cabalgan las Musas de la Poesía
espoleando profundo los flancos de la creación

gimiendo
dando a luz
al arte inmortal de escribir.

Blink of Day

... when the long darkness slides away
light changes everything. Katherine L. Gordon
The slender misty city. Archibald Lampman

dawn overflows,
a misty window face-like drawing
slowly drips down the glass
distinct contours becoming
a trickle;
now a hazy
masked bead mimic
hiding in the sill

glints replace shadows
roosters replace crickets

the tempting aroma of freshly-baked bread
wafting up from the bakery down the corner
blends with earth´s scents
and nips my taste buds

– a nook of bedroom silence is chipped by the
alarm clock´s boisterous reveille –

light lands upon the city, darkness deferred
another 12 hours

blink of day in my eyes

Pestañeo del día

… cuando la demorada oscuridad se va
la luz lo cambia todo. Katherine L. Gordon
La tenue borrosa ciudad. Archibald Lampman

el alba se desborda,
el dibujo que parece un rostro en la ventana empañada
se escurre lentamente por el cristal
contornos claros se van convirtiendo
en un chorro;
ahora una imprecisa
mímica de gota enmascarada
escondiéndose en el alféizar

los destellos sustituyen a las sombras
los gallos sustituyen a los grillos

el aroma tentador de pan recién horneado
llega desde la panadería en la esquina
se mezcla con el romance perfumado de la tierra
y mordisquea mis papilas gustativas

– un recodo de silencio en la habitación es astillado por la
llamada ruidosa del reloj despertador –

la luz se posa sobre la ciudad, la oscuridad postergada
otras 12 horas

pestañeo del día en mis ojos

Rivers

Until your tears join us in a rainbow. Bernice Lever
The fertile germination of a sentient breath. John B. Lee

life beats out there muffled
by glass windows
a river of motion, sounds bouncing back
dimmed and distant,
a collage of stories
expanding perpetually
 like the galaxy

in here, you and I
have mapped our anatomies more than once
heard the racing rumble
of our bloodstream;

we meant to be silent but
lost control over words
spelt them in gasps
weeps
groans

infinite pleasure seeping through the skin
life in us, syllables stuttered
bodies heaving
tremors in harmony with
 the Universe

a river of two surging
towards the finish.

Ríos

Hasta que tus lágrimas nos unan en un arco iris. Bernice Lever
El fecundo brote de un aliento sentimental. John B. Lee

la vida palpita allá afuera, amortiguada
por ventanas de cristal
un río de movimiento, sonidos que rebotan
tenues y distantes,
un collage de historias
expandiéndose perpetuas
como la galaxia

aquí dentro, tú y yo
hemos visitado nuestra anatomía más de una vez
escuchado el fragor apresurado
de nuestra sangre;

quisimos estar en silencio pero
perdimos el control de las palabras
las deletreadas en jadeos
 sollozos
 gemidos

placer infinito filtrándose por la piel
la vida en nosotros, sílabas balbuceadas
 cuerpos suspirando
temblores en sintonía con
el Universo

un río de dos en oleada
hacia la meta.

The First Day

The first day. Genesis 1:5
As the first day. Bernice Lever
To feel the pulse of life. Malca Litovitz and Elana Wolff

like the new sun rising
and the sea renewing itself in wavy romance
with the shore
leaving runic signs on the sand,
I breathe in the pulse of life

awake at this hour in the sleepy waterside
I calibrate my existence as I surf
with the tide
weigh my crests and shallows
skin-deep essences retained
substantialunrepeated

I interpret
ocean messages of long ago
cosmic capsules
wherein life was rocketed to earth
and expanded sea to land
from natural noise to sentient sound

this is where I stand,
before the primordial source.

God divided light from darkness,

my eyes receive awakening
this pulse of life refreshed
to embrace me
like *the first day* of all creation.

El primer día

El primer día. Génesis 1:5
Como el primer día. Bernice Lever
Para sentir el pulso de la vida. Malca Litovitz y Elana Wolff

como el nuevo sol despuntando
y el mar renovándose en romance ondulante
con la costa
dejando signos misteriosos sobre la arena,
respiro la pulsación de la vida

despierto a esta hora en la orilla soñolienta
calibro mi existencia mientras navego
con la marea
pondero mis crestas y mis simas
esencias a flor de piel retenidas
significativasirrepetibles

interpreto
mensajes oceánicos de antaño
cápsulas cósmicas
donde la vida fue lanzada a la tierra
y se expandió del mar a la tierra
del ruido natural al sonido consciente

es aquí donde estoy parado,
ante de la fuente primordial.

Dios dividió la luz de las tinieblas,

mis ojos reciben el despertar
esta pulsación de vida renovada
para abrazarme
como *el primer día* de toda la creación.

Lucky

To my wife
You and I sit staring. Kimberley Grove

Once more our welcome habit,
we sit on the porch
and wave the night hello.

You sip your coffee
proudly display for me
the nightgown you know is my favorite
and speak of tomorrow
so passionately
I can almost touch it with my eyes.

We gaze into the night
a zillion worlds twinkle up there
their traveling beams come mildly down
to glint in your eyes.

Once more the time is perfect
to realize how lucky I was
to find you.

Afortunado

A mi esposa
Tú y yo sentados contemplamos. Kimberley Grove

Una vez más nuestra grata costumbre,
nos sentamos en el portal
y saludamos la noche.

Tomas un sorbo de café
orgullosa me muestras
la bata de casa que sabes es mi favorita
y hablas del mañana
tan apasionadamente
que casi puedo tocarlo con mis ojos.

Atisbamos la noche
una infinidad de mundos destellan allá arriba
sus haces de luz viajeros descienden suavemente
para reflejarse en tus ojos.

Una vez más es el momento perfecto
para darme cuenta de cuán afortunado fui
al encontrarte.

Beyond the Tyranny of Time

To my father
Tomorrow the sun will rise again. Tom Hanks (in Cast Away)
... this is my father. A. F. Moritz
... so that you guide me, dear father. Wency Rosales

The sun gloriously shines upon my father´s
bald head this morning. He reads Agatha Christie
placidly seated on his favorite rocking chair
that I put in the patio following
his instructions to the letter that the sun
must reach his back, warm him, activate his tired skin.
Eighty-four is so easy to say yet so hard for him
to handle physically: dependent on his walker
it takes him an eternity to go from his room
to the patio. His mind intact though,
which he trains and trains solving crossword puzzles
rereading old books, keeping phone numbers
in his brain, buying newspapers and magazines
tirelessly watching series and films.
Out on the street life goes by, as has his own
even if now it does not seem so long
because we know his journey is silently
coming to an end. I wonder if
he ever fancies he is with Mom again,
who left us fifteen years ago and waits
somewhere over the rainbow for him to join her.
At night in the next room, I hear his sighs
and complaints: the pain in his leg
is punishing him despite injections, ointments
and my tireless sister´s loving care...

Father, the sun will shine again tomorrow
life will go on and your rocking chair will always welcome you
beyond the ungracious tyranny of time.

Más allá de la tiranía del tiempo

A mi padre
Mañana el sol saldrá otra vez. Tom Hanks (en Náufrago)
… este es mi padre. A. F. Moritz
… para que me guíes, querido padre. Wency Rosales

El sol brilla espléndido sobre la desnuda cabeza
de mi padre esta mañana. Lee Agatha Christie
plácidamente sentado en su balance favorito
que puse en el patio siguiendo
sus instrucciones al pie de la letra de que el sol
llegara a su espalda, lo calentara, activara su cansada piel.
Es fácil decir ochenta y cuatro mas es difícil para él
lidiar con ello físicamente: dependiente de su andador
le toma una eternidad ir de su cuarto
al patio. Su mente intacta sin embargo,
la cual entrena y entrena resolviendo crucigramas
releyendo viejos libros, reteniendo números telefónicos
en su cerebro, comprando periódicos y revistas
viendo incansable seriales y películas.
Afuera en la calle la vida sigue, como ha hecho la suya
incluso si ahora no parece tan larga
porque sabemos que su travesía está llegando
silenciosamente a su final. Me pregunto si
a veces imagina que está con Mamá de nuevo,
quien nos dejó hace quince años y espera
en algún lugar al otro lado del arcoiris que vaya a su encuentro.
De noche en la habitación al lado, oigo sus suspiros
y quejas: el dolor en su pierna
lo está castigando a pesar de las inyecciones, las pomadas
y el amoroso cuidado de mi incansable hermana…

Padre, el sol brillará nuevamente mañana
la vida continuará y tu balance siempre te recibirá
más allá de la penosa tiranía del tiempo.

Sisterly Gift

To my sister, Vivian

When I was born my sister
welcomed me as her "little toy brother,"
one she´d rush in from school
wash her hands to tend to
and play with for hours and hours.
I remember her cuddling me and giving me her love
that has lasted through the years.
It was always like that, she'd be there for me,
still is, the more mature sibling watching over
the younger one, taking him to and back from school back then
supporting me through hard times now...

I carry with me her undisputed fortitude
the softness of her voice
the sweet, calm smile when I visit
and stay overnight and she regales me with her kindness
and her cuisine (despite her dislike of cooking)
that reminds me of our mother.
On our final stretch of life, I thank God
for the sisterly gift
He generously, wisely had for me
when I uttered my first cry coming into the world.

Regalo de Hermana

A mi hermana, Vivian

Cuando nací mi hermana
me recibió como su "pequeño hermano de juguete",
por quien ella vendría apresurada de la escuela
lavaría sus manos para atenderlo
y jugaría con él por horas y horas.
La recuerdo abrazándome y dándome su amor
que ha durado por años.
Siempre fue así, estaría ahí para mí,
aún lo está, la hermana más madura cuidando
al más joven, llevándolo y trayéndolo de la escuela en aquel entonces
apoyándome en momentos difíciles ahora…

Llevo conmigo su fortaleza innegable
la suavidad de su voz
la sonrisa dulce y calmada cuando la visito
y me quedo hasta el otro día y me regala su bondad
y su estilo de cocinar (a pesar de no gustarle la cocina)
que me recuerda a nuestra madre.
En nuestro tramo final en la vida, agradezco a Dios
por el regalo de hermana
que Él generosamente, sabiamente tenía para mí
cuando di mi primer grito al venir al mundo.

Lebensraum

The rustle of the wild
whispers from both sides of the highway,
beckoning undertones reaching out
to tempt me. I halt, briefly,
lured by a dim glimmer of sunrise
sneaking through the shrubbery, scurry
sounds of cautious creatures I can´t see
dart away from a trespassing human.
They fear the camera
its sudden flash breaching, snooping into
their privacies and liberties where
they reign unaware of the subjugation
of time or the quicksand of lies. I turn around.
In deference to their lebensraum
suddenly dawned on me, I forget about
my photo and let them be.

Espacio vital

El crujido de la naturaleza
murmura desde ambos lados de la autopista,
matiz de susurros llegando a mí
para tentarme. Me detengo, brevemente,
cautivado por un ligero resplandor de amanecer
que se filtra entre los arbustos, sonidos
apresurados de criaturas cautelosas que no puedo ver
se alejan precipitadamente de un humano que transgrede.
Le temen a la cámara
su destello repentino irrumpiendo, husmeando en
su privacidad y libertades donde
reinan sin saber lo que es la sumisión
del tiempo o las arenas movedizas de las mentiras. Doy la vuelta.
Por respeto a su espacio vital
del que de repente me doy cuenta, me olvido de
mi foto y las dejo en paz.

Days roll slowly by

Thank you, Antony Di Nardo...

Days roll slowly by
conquering the distance between
sunrise and sunset. I don´t know
how to measure it,
just stare and wonder
at what invisible sky fountains
sun and clouds and wind pause
to quench their thirst
as they cross
the cycles of time.

Los días transcurren lentos

Gracias, Antony Di Nardo

Los días transcurren lentos
conquistando la distancia entre
la salida y la puesta del sol. No sé
cómo medirla,
solo observo y me pregunto
en qué invisibles fuentes del cielo
el sol y las nubes y el viento se detienen
a saciar su sed
mientras cruzan
los ciclos del tiempo.

Even in the Rain

What can we do with the rain? James Deahl
... a blood pulse in the drumming dark. John B. Lee

Darkening skycanvas looms
beyond the window
fistfuls of angry clouds float windward
as hearts on earth leap
uncertain
blood jet-pumped –
lovers' attention
diverted for a second;

every bloodstream quickens
on the brink of storm.

Imminence only a thunderbolt away
from bursting into
gusts of rain,
we pause awed by the sight.

But then you nudge me and wink
to reclaim the attention you deserve

even in the rain.

Incluso en la lluvia

¿Qué podemos hacer con la lluvia? James Deahl
… un pulso de sangre en la rasgueante oscuridad. John B. Lee

Lienzo celeste se asoma
más allá de la ventana
puñados de nubes airadas flotan con el viento
mientras los corazones en la tierra saltan
inseguros
la sangre bombeada con fuerza —
la atención de los amantes
desviada por un instante;

todos los flujos sanguíneos se aceleran
a punto de una tormenta.

Lo inminente solo a un rayo de distancia
de explotar en
ráfagas de lluvia,
hacemos una pausa sobrecogidos por el espectáculo.

Me tocas suavemente con el codo y me guiñas un ojo
para reclamar la atención que te mereces

incluso en la lluvia.

Poljot

To my paternal grandparents, Enrique and Zeida
And felt my heart hum. Don Gutteridge

Today I found my old analog watch,
Poljot (Russian for *flight*).

It was in my lowest chest drawer
dusty cracked glass, opaque green hands
missing their journeys around the digits. My heart leapt.

It was a gift from my grandparents when I was nine,
You have good grades, they approved with a smile,
We certainly hope it stays long with you, they decreed sternly
with their 1970s-grandparent style.

My watch glowed in the dark,
I'd spend nights smelling the black leather bracelet
looking at its glass cover under my bed sheets, marveled,
trying to notice the minute hand's
unnoticeable silent movement…

My grandparents' demise came long before
my watch stopped for good. I was able to honor
their wish: it stayed with me until
no watchmaker could fix it.

That's when I put it in my drawer till today.
For a second it ticked fond family memories back to me

and this poem took *flight* from my drawer.

Poljot

Hoy encontré mi viejo reloj analógico,
Poljot (*vuelo* en ruso).

Estaba en la última gaveta de mi cómoda
cristal polvoriento cuarteado, manecillas verdes opacas
echando de menos a sus viajes alrededor de los dígitos. Mi corazón saltó.

Fue un regalo de mis abuelos cuando tenía nueve años,
Sacas buenas notas, admitieron con una sonrisa,
Evidentemente esperamos que te dure bastante, decretaron firmemente
con su estilo de abuelos de los años 70.

Mi reloj brillaba en la oscuridad,
me pasaba noches oliendo la pulsera de cuero negro
mirando su cubierta de cristal bajo mis sábanas, maravillado,
tratando de distinguir el indistinguible movimiento silencioso
del minutero…

El fallecimiento de mis abuelos ocurrió mucho antes
de que mi reloj se parara definitivamente. Pude honrar
su deseo: permaneció conmigo hasta que
ningún relojero pudo arreglarlo.

Fue entonces que lo puse en mi gaveta hasta hoy.
Por un instante su tic-tac trajo de vuelta tiernos recuerdos de familia

y este poema alzó *vuelo* desde mi gaveta.

Afterkiss

… secret honeyed kisses. Norma West Linder
A kiss is just a kiss. Billie Holiday

An afterkiss lingers
in the pleasure-soaked shadows
warm like embers, incomplete
like dusk pilfering the sun´s
bits of farewell light, fantasizing
about second chances
with mute pouts—evoking. An afterkiss
tickles the nude skin, yearning
sketching a billet-doux with wishful lips
that circle, circle, circle
until the shadows burn again.

Post-beso

... secretos besos melosos. Norma West Linder
Un beso es simplemente un beso. Billie Holiday

Un post-beso persevera
en las sombras colmadas de placer
cálido como ascuas, inconcluso
como un crepúsculo que hurta del sol
retazos de luz de despedida, fantaseando
sobre segundas oportunidades
con mohines silenciosos—sugerentes. Un post-beso
cosquillea la piel desnuda, anhelante
esbozando una nota amorosa con labios deseosos
que rondan, rondan, rondan
hasta que las sombras arden de nuevo.

Silence

... the selfsame fertile silence. Allan Briesmaster
... a subtle moment of silence before the pens
start scratching. Don Gutteridge
... where silence is the light the poem shadows from. John B. Lee

Silence blesses midnight
above my roof. It carries a blanket
spreading it over the buildings. Silence
taps hellos on my window
and speaks to me with voiceless words
that leap to my desk.

Silence then smiles
goodbye and floats away

to another home.

El silencio

… el propio silencio fértil. Allan Briesmaster
… un sublime momento de silencio antes que las plumas
comiencen a raspear. Don Gutteridge
… donde el silencio es la luz de la que emerge el poema. John B. Lee

El silencio bendice la medianoche
sobre mi techo. Viene con una manta
extendiéndola sobre los edificios. El silencio
golpea suavemente saludos en mi ventana
y me habla con palabras mudas
que saltan a mi escritorio.

El silencio sonríe entonces
un adiós y flota alejándose

hasta otro hogar.

Never More

... to sleep; no more... William Shakespeare
... ah, nevermore! Edgar Allan Poe
Underneath these thoughts. Sarah Richardson

A dawn of cars
derails
my
thoughts
of
 you, tows
them chaotically away.

A brief silence falls
no horns blared
no tires screeched.

For a minute thoughts return,
a damp silhouette
of skin, lips,

eyes. Like dawn, dewed – intangible...

Absence is a guest; best room for her.
Same room *we slept* together. Never more.

Nunca más

... dormir; no más... William Shakespeare
... ¡ah, nunca más! Edgar Allan Poe
Bajo estos pensamientos. Sarah Richardson

Un amanecer de automóviles
descarrila
mis
pensamientos
de
ti, los remolca
caóticamente lejos.

Un breve silencio llega
no resuenan las bocinas
no chirrean las gomas.

Por un minuto los pensamientos retornan,
una amortecida silueta
de piel, labios,

ojos. Como el amanecer, cubierta de rocío – intangible...

La ausencia es un huésped; la mejor habitación para ella.
La misma donde *dormimos* juntos. Nunca más.

2020 into 21:
Trump into Biden

In collaboration with Richard Grove

A new era for US
and by extension for Cuba
and further into the world,
our expectations
are focused on the now
from yesterday on.

Biden's speech weaves
promising threads of hope
and reassurance for many,
including us
on our island
90 miles south of Florida.

This inaugural event
plus the Cuban vaccine
about to be dispersed
island-wide will be
the beginning of the answers
to our prayers for recovery,
and a dawn of relief
for our macro and our
personal budgets.

We see in Biden's words
the gossamer of hope
a semblance of truth
the expectation of unity.
Let us pray he does not speak
with rhetorical lies, spilling
more brutality and measures
that try to choke us. Let us pray
he honors the rebuilding
that Obama started:

A new era for both sides.

De 2020 a 2021:
de Trump hacia Biden

En colaboración con Richard Grove

Una nueva era para los Estados Unidos
y por extensión para Cuba
y más allá en el mundo,
nuestras expectativas
se concentran en el ahora
desde ayer en adelante.

El discurso de Biden trenza
hilos promisorios de esperanza
y consuelo para muchos,
incluidos nosotros
en nuestra isla
90 millas al sur de la Florida.

Este evento inaugural
más la vacuna cubana
a punto de ser aplicada
en toda la isla será
el inicio de las respuestas
a nuestras oraciones de recuperación,
y un amanecer de alivio
para nuestros presupuestos
macro y personales.

Vemos en las palabras de Biden
el delicado tejido de esperanza
una apariencia de verdad
la expectativa de unidad.
Roguemos que no hable
con mentiras retóricas, vertiendo
más brutalidad y medidas
que intentan ahogarnos. Roguemos
que honre la reedificación
que comenzó Obama:

Una nueva era para ambas partes.

Collage

... lights of the sky. Eva Kolacz
White light descending, wrap me in peace. Elana Wolff

I hold a sheaf of peaceful dawn
in my hand,
squeeze it gently. Drops of white-blue
trickle through my fingers:

A collage of light
and my tropes.

Collage

... luces del cielo. Eva Kolacz
Blanca luz que desciendes, rodéame de paz. Elana Wolff

Sostengo un haz de sosegado amanecer
en mi mano,
lo aprieto suavemente. Gotas de blanco-azul
manan por entre mis dedos:

Un collage de luz
y mis tropos.

Raingift

To my wife
After the pizzicato rains. Henry Beissel
That rainbow in the distance. Robert A. Boates
Coiled in embrace. Fran Figge

After the rain
the gift of transparency,
a sky bathed in light
letting the sun dry it
intimately, warmly;
yet not before it showered its host of beads
upon the grateful land.

Then
a rainbow over the city
the return of chirping
people and their skeptical umbrellas
reappearing in the streets

and us,
as grateful as the land
warm
bathed in light and life

embraced.

Regalo de lluvia

A mi esposa
Después de las lluvias en pizicato. Henry Beissel
Ese arco iris a lo lejos. Robert A. Boates
Entrelazados en un abrazo. Fran Figge

Después de la lluvia
la dádiva de la claridad,
un cielo bañado en luz
dejando que el sol lo seque
íntimamente, cálidamente;
no sin antes haber derramado su multitud de gotas
sobre la tierra agradecida.

Luego
un arco iris sobre la ciudad
el regreso de los gorjeos
la gente y sus paraguas suspicaces
reapareciendo en las calles

y nosotros,
tan agradecidos como la tierra
cálidos
bañados en luz y vida

abrazados.

Aroma

To my father
Father, when I think of you. John Tyndall
... so kind and decent like my father. Tom Hamilton

From time to time
from my mother´s rocking chair
or my father´s writing desk,
I´d spy on Dad
watch him smoke his long cigars, inhale in sheer
pleasure and expertise,
their aroma spreading
in the room as he fumed out from his nostrils...

I would cough then and he would discover me
crush his cigar, draw me near
sit me on his lap
and smile his perfect white smile
in a warm hug,
mild tobacco scent
lingering in the room – and still in my mind

some forty-five
years later.

Aroma

A mi padre
Padre, cuando pienso en ti. John Tyndall
… tan amable y decente como mi padre. Tom Hamilton

Algunas veces
desde el balance de mi madre
o el escritorio de mi padre,
yo espiaba a papá
lo veía fumar sus largos tabacos, inhalar con total
placer y pericia,
su aroma expandiéndose
por la habitación mientras echaba humo por su nariz…

entonces yo tosía y él me descubría
aplastaba su tabaco, me acercaba a él
me sentaba en su regazo
y sonreía su blanca sonrisa perfecta
con un abrazo cálido,
suave olor a tabaco
persistiendo en la habitación – y todavía en mi mente

unos cuarenta y cinco
años después.

Clash

As the storm approaches. James Deahl
... storm clouds loom low. Norma West Linder

The gloom-packed lethargy
of the sky
weighs many a ton on the city´s
shoulders. Grey clouds
march somber and martial
over hurrying crowds
and shutting windows. It looks like
heavy rain
in this shrouded afternoon,
thunder deafening
lightning chiseling the nearby hills.
Dead calm hangs awhile in the air
presaging a storm
that´ll raid and ravage helpless
life caught outdoors in the impending clash
of water and earth.

June 17, 2021

Colisión

Mientras se acerca la tormenta. James Deahl
… nubes de tormenta bajas en la lejanía. Norma West Linder

El letargo cargado de penumbra
en el cielo
pesa enormemente en los hombros
de la ciudad. Nubes grises
marchan sombrías y marciales
sobre multitudes apuradas
y ventanas que se cierran. Parece
que va a diluviar
en esta amortajada tarde.,
truenos ensordecedores
relámpagos cincelando las colinas cercanas.
Calma total flota por un rato en el aire
presagiando una tormenta
que atacará y asolará la indefensa
vida atrapada a la intemperie en la inminente colisión
del agua y la tierra.

Junio 17, 2021

Past the Night Rest

By mighty dreams possessed… Bliss Carman
Safe in bed you may dream. Raymond Souster

Past the night rest our hearts
lighten their yesterday weight
beat cheerfully restored
to face what is to come
after a dream-walk down memory lane.
Collages of people, experiences gathered
flash like a movie: we star
in our own story unfolding in images
spun in our brains
that oftentimes baffle us yet teach or warn
or show the way to leave with us
a web of questions
a wonder frown
a resolute, hopeful smile at
the new day ahead
of challenge and reward.

Luego del reposo nocturno

Poseídos por sueños poderosos… Bliss Carman
Protegido en cama puedes dormir. Raymond Souster

Luego del reposo nocturno nuestros corazones
se aligeran de su lastre del ayer
laten alegremente repuestos
para enfrentar lo que ha de venir
después de un sueño-paseo por la senda del recuerdo.
Collages de gente, experiencias acumuladas
deslumbran como una película: somos los protagonistas
en nuestra propia historia revelada en imágenes
tejidas en nuestros cerebros
que muchas veces nos confunden mas enseñan o alertan
o muestran el camino para dejar con nosotros
una urdimbre de preguntas
un fruncido ceño de asombro
una decidida, esperanzada sonrisa para
el nuevo día por llegar
de reto y recompensa.

I have seen

Woman, in a dream of desire I have come... John B. Lee
Woman, I can hardly express... John Lennon

I have seen the wake of night
dissolve in the rising ember of morning
I have breathed it briefly down my alveoli
their shudder with me through the instant
my anima rejoicing, synapses
inscribing the moment. I have watched too
the day's downfall. End hour, yet majestic
in its gala hues, fireworks
igniting and flaring the way they only do
in your irises' diamond veins.

He visto

Mujer, en un sueño de deseo he venido… John B. Lee
Mujer, no puedo casi decir… John Lennon

He visto la estela de la noche
disolverse en las brasas nacientes de la mañana
la he respirado brevemente hasta mis alveolos
su tremor junto a mí a través del instante
mi alma regocijada, las sinapsis
guardando el momento. He observado también
el declive del día. Hora final, pero majestuosa
en sus matices de gala, fuegos artificiales
iluminando y prendiéndose de la forma que solo lo hacen
en las venas de diamante de tus iris.

Stop-off

... to the great beyond. Marvin Orbach
... a dove this morning... outside my window. Antony Di Nardo

A dove flies past my window
cooing her way through,
poses gently on an antenna anchored
in the nearby building´s rooftop teeming
with a flock of her flight mates
that parade in noisy bunches.
She cranes her neck in cue noes. Probably disapproval,
denial; maybe concern or simply adjustment.
She flaps her wings, a shudder of elegance
that stirs the air sending some feather castoffs
down as if willing to sign
her transient presence on the roof
before her partners line up, eager to end
the visit, and soar en route
to an appealing blue-white vastness.

Escala

... hacia el extenso más allá. Marvin Orbach
... una paloma esta mañana... frente a mi ventana. Antony Di Nardo

Una paloma pasa volando frente a mi ventana
arrullando en su camino,
se posa suavemente en una antena sujeta
a la azotea del edificio cercano colmada
de una bandada de sus compañeras de vuelo
que desfilan en ruidosos grupos.
Estira el cuello en señales de censura. Tal vez rechazo,
negación; quizás preocupación o simplemente ajuste.
Mueve sus alas, un temblor de elegancia
que agita el aire mandando algunos restos de plumas
al suelo como si deseara firmar
su efímera presencia en el techo
antes de que sus amigas formen, ansiosas de terminar
la visita, y asciendan en dirección
a una atrayente inmensidad azul-blanca.

Here for You

To my daughter, Amanda
There is no here without you. Paul Carr

My watch has stopped
on your time-string. It means
it is *here, now*
my longest pause
to live for you.

Here, where my heart beats
now, when it beats

only
for you.

Aquí para ti

Para mi hija, Amanda
No hay aquí sin ti. Paul Carr

Mi reloj se ha detenido
en tu cuerda temporal. Eso quiere decir
que es *aquí*, *ahora*
mi más larga pausa
para vivir para ti.

Aquí, donde late mi corazón
ahora, cuando late

solo
para ti.

Magnificence

thirty-three-thousand shades of green. John B. Lee
The sky exposed. Antony Di Nardo
It's all nature. Antony Di Nardo

Life is best enjoyed
from my vantage point:

blue sky like a tablecloth ready to be set
upon the hilltops

green mat extending far beyond
my eyescope

cosmopolitan trees basking in the sunny canvas
where the vista of the city bows

before nature's magnificence.

Magnificencia

treinta y tres mil matices de verde. John B. Lee
El cielo develado. Antony Di Nardo
Todo es la naturaleza. Antony Di Nardo

La vida se disfruta mejor
desde mi ventajosa posición:

cielo azul como un mantel listo para ser colocado
sobre las cimas de las colinas

alfombra verde que se extiende mucho más allá
de donde alcanzan mis ojos

árboles cosmopolitas tomando sol en el radiante lienzo
donde la vista de la ciudad se inclina

ante la magnificencia de la naturaleza.

Motif in my Soul

... the poems that visit my desk and flow through my pen.
I am simply a vessel, and I am thankful when the muses visit.
John B. Lee
... the perpetual prism of a poem. Don Gutteridge

Oftentimes I have considered
what prods a motif in my soul,
that sudden tremor felt in the moment
my eyes devour a poem,
sparkled as they chance
upon a perfect line, a candid remark
a suggestive twist, a splendid metaphor.
Oftentimes I have wondered
what undercurrents or muses
unleash the urge, the rush, the spur
that make my hand become a vessel
and a poem, its course.

Motivo en mi alma

... los poemas que visitan mi escritorio y fluyen a través de mi pluma.
Soy simplemente un medio, y agradezco cuando las musas me visitan.
John B. Lee
... el eterno prisma de un poema. Don Gutteridge

Con frecuencia he ponderado
qué incita un motivo en mi alma,
ese tremor repentino que se siente en el momento
en que mis ojos devoran un poema,
encendidos cuando se encuentran
con una línea perfecta, una frase sincera
un giro sugerente, una impresionante metáfora.
Con frecuencia me he preguntado
qué trasfondos o musas
desencadenan el impulso, el ímpetu, el acicate
que hacen que mi mano se vuelva un navío
y un poema, su rumbo.

Harbinger of Rain

Rain thumped a thousand million urgent fists
against the shingles. John B. Lee
The rain so strong. Richard Grove
And rainstorms, too—always rain lancing... James Deahl

Where heavy clouds kiss the hilltops
a line zigzags
like a river of grey light about to overflow,
harbinger of rain
upon the city below.

Thunder bursts in clicks and roar
lightning precedes it cracking the skycrystal
bolt-scarring the shrouded dome
for an infinitesimal lapse
of looming clarity.

Lilliputian raindrops venture down, chilly scouters
paving the way for their cyclopean siblings,
a frozen grid of buildings and streets
receives the downpour,
a concert of splashing, gurgling, tinkling
spreads and raids onto
outdoor life, architecture, whatever little motion
is left while rain plummets
with its water spears, its bucketfuls of flood
covering the vulnerable land.

Heraldo de la lluvia

La lluvia golpeó un billón de puños apremiantes
contra las tejas. John B. Lee
La lluvia tan fuerte. Richard Grove
Y temporales, también—siempre la lluvia lanceando. James Deahl

Donde las nubes cargadas besan las cimas montañosas
una línea zigzaguea
como un río de luz gris a punto de desbordarse,
un heraldo de la lluvia
sobre la ciudad allá abajo.

Truenos estallan en chasquidos y estruendos
el relampagueo les precede cuarteando el cristal celeste
dejando una cicatriz de rayos en el oscuro domo
por un lapso infinitesimal
de claridad amenazante.

Liliputienses gotas de lluvia se aventuran, exploradoras álgidas
que preparan el camino para sus ciclópeas hermanas,
un entramado de edificios y calles
recibe el aguacero,
un concierto de salpicaduras, borboteos, tintineos
se expande y asalta
la vida exterior, la arquitectura, cualquier pequeño movimiento
que quede mientras la lluvia cae en picada
con sus lanzas de agua, sus puñados de diluvio
cubriendo la vulnerable tierra.

April rain

... a rainy spring day. Richard Grove
Rain terminates our long dry spell. James Deahl
... what comes with rain. John B. Lee

Clouds look like
grey whales pregnant with water,
grumbles an elderly lady watching
April rain fall whimsically first on the southbound
lanes of the Holguin beltway,
roaming fast downtown
in its debut downpour of the year.
After months of drought, the skies open
with unusual silence, no thunder or lightning
only the vertical curtain of cold beads
hardly wind-skewed.
Grass cheers—lawns and gardens will green;
hedges gurgle now under the shower
the neighbor´s lilies explain their perfume
with wet utterances that tell
about the joys of the arriving season.

Lluvia de abril

… un lluvioso día de primavera. Richard Grove
La lluvia pone fin a nuestra larga sequía. James Deahl
… lo que viene con la lluvia. John B. Lee

Las nubes parecen
ballenas grises embarazadas de agua,
se queja una señora mayor viendo
la lluvia de abril caer caprichosa primero sobre la autopista
sur de la circunvalación de Holguín,
desplazándose rápidamente al centro del pueblo
en su aguacero debut del año.
Luego de meses de sequía, los cielos se abren
con un silencio inusual, sin truenos ni relámpagos
solo la cortina vertical de frías gotas
casi ni inclinadas por el viento.
La hierba se anima—prados y jardines reverdecerán;
los setos borbotean ahora bajo el chaparrón
los lirios de la vecina explican su perfume
con expresiones húmedas que hablan
de los júbilos de la estación que llega.

Rain-gazer

... what comes with rain. John B. Lee
Rain, the wet refrain. Elana Wolff

Rain knocks tuneful and inviting
at my window,
jingle music plays along post-written in damp
symbols trickling
 down to
a sill's hospitality
that I decode: some sort of unexpected blessing
come to me
to read chink-clues falling ruled by gravity's
inescapable grip.
Moments of solace. Me, a rain-gazer peeking
through the bead strings and
impromptu street rivulets,
conjuring soaked words up
so I can delineate *to the letter*
nature's language of tears.

Espectador de la lluvia

… lo que viene con la lluvia. John B. Lee
Lluvia, el húmedo estribillo. Elana Wolff

La lluvia toca melodiosa y tentadora
a mi ventana,
música en repique suena de seguido post-escrita en húmedos
símbolos que gotean
hasta
una hospitalidad de alféizar
que descifro: algún tipo de bendición inesperada
venida a mí
para leer tintineos-signos que caen regidos por el inevitable
dominio de la gravedad.
Momentos de paz. Yo, un espectador de la lluvia atisbando
a través de los hilos de gotas y l
os improvisados riachuelos en las calles,
invocando palabras empapadas
para poder delinear *al pie de la letra*
el lenguaje de lágrimas de la naturaleza.

Tongues of the Ocean

... and the gathered waters he called "seas." Genesis 1:10
... to an unknown ocean. John B. Lee
The cool, green ocean. Richard Grove
What is it about the ocean? Kim Grove

Here I stand upon an inconstant, undulating line
drawn by the bold tongues of the ocean
soft-lapping the sand,
age-old event-remodeler of earth, lung-like
marine renewal
exchanging blueness/greenness
over fine-grained rock. Sensations of gratitude visit
as sinuous as the hieroglyphs carved
unyielding warm wetness
massaging my bare feet
a mind-healing
airborne primeval version of algae, corals
salting my nostrils. Liquid silence prompting me
to envision
the enigmatic abyss beyond –
 below. Ocean mumbles
wave-symbols, speaks in rippled idioms skipping from
surf-crest-to-surf-crest.
Low tide bids farewell; high tide surges in
imposing its voice of water on lovers´ only recently written,
short-lived words
rinsed away by replicating tongues
never ceasing to roll in upon the seashore, never relinquishing
their regal station, their licking-sweeping
their sculpting role beneath
a contemplative sky.

Lenguas del océano

… y a la reunión de lasaguas llamó Mares. Génesis 1:10
… hacia un mar desconocido. John B. Lee
El fresco, verde océano. Richard Grove
¿Qué tiene el océano? Kim Grove

Aquí estoy de pie sobre una cambiante, ondulante línea
trazada por las atrevidas lenguas del océano
lamiendo suavemente la arena,
inmemorial remodelador de sucesos de la tierra, renovación marina
como un pulmón
intercambiando azul/verde
sobre roca de finos granos. Sensaciones de gratitud visitan
tan sinuosas como los jeroglíficos tallados
tenaces una tibia humedad
masajeando mis pies descalzos
una sanadora de la mente
versión prístina llevada por el aire de algas, corales
salando mis fosas nasales. Silencio líquido incitándome
a vislumbrar
el enigmático abismo más allá –
debajo. El océano murmura
oleajes-símbolos, habla en idiomas de ondas que rebotan de
ola-cresta a ola-cresta.
La bajamar dice adiós; la pleamar se abalanza
imponiendo su voz de agua sobre las recién escritas,
efímeras palabras de los amantes
lavadas por lenguas replicándose
que nunca cesan de venir hasta la orilla, nunca renuncian
a su regio estatus, su chapaleo-barrido
su rol de esculpido bajo
un meditabundo cielo.

All in the Day's Eye

… the beauty of another day. Sarah Richardson
The sun sinks closing the day. Norma West Linder

Warm afternoon breath
upon the nearby cedars. They purr knowing
the wind recalls the gentility of their crowns
how unbridled it can blow
through leaves and branches
translate its whistling as lovers' murmur
spelt straight into
the beauty of the day's blinking eye.

      … An elder sun departs from earth. An eagle soars
undaunted, mistress of airspace
scanning targets she might raid onto
in the imminent shade
gliding in the wind that quits the trees unwillingly
anticipating her sustenance as soon as dusk
whispers through the cedar grid
and naive creatures venture
into the day's closed eye.

Todo en el ojo del día

... la belleza de un nuevo día. Sarah Richardson
El sol se hunde cerrando el día. Norma West Linder

Soplo cálido de una tarde
sobre los cedros cercanos. Ronronean conscientes de que
el viento recuerda la gentileza de sus copas
cuán libre puede soplar
por entre las hojas y las ramas
traducir su silbido como murmullo de amantes
deletreado directamente en
la belleza del ojo parpadeante del día.

       ... Un sol antiguo abandona la tierra. Un águila vuela
intrépida, señora del espacio aéreo
explorando objetivos que podría asaltar
en la inminente sombra
planeando en el viento que abandona a disgusto los árboles
anticipando su sustento tan pronto como el crepúsculo
susurre a través del entramado de cedros
y criaturas ingenuas se aventuren
hacia el ojo cerrado del día.

This summer´s kick

… the rooftop lingering heat of a Cuban day. Richard Grove
… the summers remain dry. James Deahl
… volumes of summer heat. John B. Lee

This summer´s kick is wild
the wind does its thing
blowing trees bare
toying with twirls
of yanked leaves and blossoms
shepherding gravid clouds to and fro,
their eagerness to water the land
ignored. I can hear the mercilessly-sunned
roof sizzle above my head
while it pleads with the clouds
to rebel against the wind
and birth a godsend of rain
so dirt is wiped clean
so the land greens
and cools down
and greenery sprouts
as a keepsake of last spring.

La pujanza de este verano

... el insistente calor de los techos en un día cubano. Richard Grove
... los veranos siguen secos. James Deahl
... caudales de calor estival. John B. Lee

La pujanza de este verano es bravía
el viento hace su parte
dejando los árboles desnudos con su soplido
jugando con remolinos
de hojas y capullos arrancados
llevando nubes grávidas de un lado a otro,
su ansia de regar la tierra
ignorada. Puedo oír el techo despiadadamente
soleado crepitar sobre mi cabeza
mientras ruega a las nubes
que se rebelen contra el viento
y den a luz una bendición de lluvia
para que limpie la suciedad
para que la tierra reverdezca
y se refresque
y la vegetación retoñe
como remembranza de la pasada primavera.

The Finest Moment

... at the moment of pausing. John B. Lee

The finest moment comes
as the sun rolls down behind the hillridge
collapsing fireball, red-yellow slow-motion plunge
leaving an iridescent wake, a promise of
a rainbow for tomorrow
when rain surrenders to it the way
poets wish.
The gentlest hour glides by
on invisible ice skates
like cosmic figure skating
that makes the heart grow fonder
hands interlocked
mute, warm accomplices in that one act
of beauty settling mildly in the mind
that'll age yet shall never
cease to have
the touch of sentience
the blessing of wonderment.

El mejor momento

… en el instante de quietud. John B. Lee

El mejor momento llega
cuando el sol rueda detrás del borde de la colina
bola de fuego colapsando, roja-azul zambullida en cámara lenta
que deja una estela centellante, una promesa de
un arco iris para mañana
cuando la lluvia se entregue a él de la forma
que anhelan los poetas.
La más gentil hora se desliza
sobre patines invisibles
como patinaje artístico
que hace que el corazón se enternezca más
manos entrecruzadas
mudas, tibias cómplices en ese tal acto
de belleza registrándose suavemente en la mente
que envejecerá pero nunca
dejará de tener
el toque de la sensibilidad
la bendición del embeleso.

Birthdays

To my daughter and my granddaughter
… the happiness of your steps. Wency Rosales
… a signal of happiness. Jorge Pérez

September strums twice
my heart´s strings. Bliss of birthdays
falls like prayed-for rain:
my daughter´s, my granddaughter´s.
Amanda, born September 10th, my teenage child;
in pride and fear I watch her outgrow
the chrysalis I secretly hoped she´d never leave,
in joy and worry I see her take longer,
farther strides from me…
Ahitana, born September 7th, my precocious
toddler, owner of the loveliest kiss
tiny sunlight of laughter, tireless trot of innocence
reflected in those lively eyes of hers…
Two meanings for my life
two inseparable pieces of me
two special beings and one month for a celebration
that never comes to an end.

Cumpleaños

A mi hija y mi nieta
… la alegría de tus pasos. Wency Rosales
… una señal de felicidad. Jorge Pérez

Septiembre rasguea doblemente
las cuerdas de mi corazón. Júbilo de cumpleaños
que cae como lluvia invocada en plegaria:
el de mi hija, el de mi nieta.
Amanda, nacida en septiembre 10, mi niña adolescente;
con orgullo y temor la veo crecer más
que la crisálida que esperé secretamente nunca dejara,
con alegría y preocupación la veo dar más largos,
más lejanos pasos desde mí…
Ahitana, nacida en septiembre 7, mi precoz
niña pequeña, dueña del más amoroso beso
diminuta luz solar de risa, incansable trote de inocencia
reflejado en sus ojos llenos de vida…
Dos sentidos para mi vida
dos partes inseparables de mí
dos seres especiales y un mes de celebración
que nunca llega a su fin.

Visit

A thing of beauty. John Keats
Moon-Lit Night. Richard Grove
… this slow dance of fractured lunar light. Glen Sorestad

Moon sliver sneaks in
through the patio´s iron-grid canopy.
She gracefully beams her way along
with queenly mien
black points on her face
and mystery signs speaking of her "other side."

The flowers in the pots quaver
moonlight is dabbed gently on them:
the moon awakens their aroma
bathes in it right before the swift seconds
slide her out of sight. A thing of beauty
visiting to lend my night
one silver, ethereal streak.

Visita

Una belleza. John Keats
Noche iluminada por la luna. Richard Grove
… esta tenue danza de quebrada luz de luna. Glen Sorestad

Una pizca de luna entra
a través del techo enrejado del patio.
Resplandece garbosamente en su camino
con pose de reina
puntos negros en su faz
y signos misteriosos que hablan de su "otro lado".

Las flores en las macetas tiemblan
luz de luna se frota suavemente en ellas:
la luna despierta su aroma
se sumerge en él justo antes de que los fugaces segundos
se la lleven fuera de la vista. Una belleza
de visita para otorgarle a mi noche
un haz de luz plateado, sutil.

There

I know places we won't be found. Taylor Swift
... a silent kiss the hurry-hearted sigh. John B. Lee
... to the secret beauty there. John B. Lee

When the world darkens
we seek shelter there, where we can't
be called or summoned, where the air
breathes clean, scented
and the stars wink in an intimate
treat of secrecy, of promises
unrevealed, juicy.

There, where silence is the sweetest sound
and your smile the perfect image
when I reach out to kiss you. There — *here now* —
your lips sigh
with a trembling *yes*.

Allí

Sé de lugares donde no nos hallarán. Taylor Swift
... un callado beso el presuroso espíritu de un suspiro. John B. Lee
... a la secreta belleza allí. John B. Lee

Cuando el mundo se oscurece
buscamos refugio allí, donde no podemos
ser hallados o convocados, donde el aire
respira límpido, fragante
y los astros guiñan en una privada
invitación de secreto, de promesas
sin revelar, deliciosas.

Allí, donde el silencio es el más tierno sonido
y tu sonrisa la imagen perfecta
cuando me acerco a besarte. Allí – *aquí ahora* –
tus labios suspiran
con un trémulo *sí*.

9:30 pm

I look at my father´s watch,
now on my wrist. It reads
9:30 pm. Some 5 years ago he gave it to me
– for the first time –
during one of his many post-op recoveries
at home. Fearing he would not make it then,
he told me to keep it. Happily,
2 days later he asked me, smiling,
to *please "lend" it to him a little longer.*
Today 9:30 pm marks exactly 3 months
since he passed away. Can´t "lend" it to him
again. Can´t have him here with me
to recall that day together and laugh.
I look at his evocative Seiko on my wrist
and smile, sadly.

November 2, 2021

9:30 p.m.

Miro el reloj de mi padre,
ahora en mi muñeca. Tiene las
9:30 p.m. Hace unos 5 años me lo dio
– por primera vez –
durante una de sus muchas convalecencias postoperatorias
en casa. Temiendo que no lo lograría ese entonces,
me dijo que me lo quedara. Felizmente,
2 días después me pidió, sonriendo,
que *por favor se lo "prestara" un poco más de tiempo.*
Hoy las 9:30 p.m. señalan exactamente 3 meses
desde que falleció. No puedo "prestárselo"
otra vez. No puedo tenerlo aquí conmigo
para recordar ese día juntos y reírnos.
Miro su evocativo Seiko en mi muñeca
y sonrío, tristemente.

Noviembre 2, 2021

Search

To my family, my second pillar
In writers block. Ed Woods
… words from the start. Elana Wolff
All day I have written words. Robert Sward

All night I sought for
meanings. Their charm to prompt me
their contours
to grant me passage
into realms of poetry. All night,

my wife asleep beside me,
next door
my stepdaughter and my step-granddaughter
gently breathe

on the other side
of Holguín my daughter rests too
in dreams of castles, heroes, fairytales…
a smile upon her lips
a peaceful sigh.

All night I have searched for these
very words.

Angels
watch over them
lighting stars
beneath their sleep-closed eyes
to bless our home
our lives.

These words I found.
The right ones.

The best ones.

Búsqueda

A mi familia, mi segundo pilar
Bloqueo de escritor. Ed Woods
… palabras desde el comienzo. Elana Wolff
Todo el día he escrito palabras. Robert Sward

Toda la noche busqué
significados. Su encanto para inspirarme
sus contornos
para darme paso
a los reinos de la poesía. Toda la noche,

mi esposa dormida a mi lado,
en la otra puerta
mi hijastra y mi nietastra
respiran suavemente

al otro lado
de Holguín mi hija descansa también
en sueños de castillos, héroes, cuentos de hadas…
una sonrisa en sus labios
un apacible suspiro.

Toda la noche he buscado estas
precisas palabras

Los ángeles
las protegen
encendiendo estrellas
bajo sus ojos cerrados por el sueño
para bendecir nuestro hogar
nuestras vidas.

Encontré estas palabras.
Las adecuadas.

Las mejores.

Afterword

A Junction of Feelings and Words: A Comprehensive Exploration of Professor Miguel Ángel Olivé Iglesias' Literary Production and Comments on his Poetry Book: *This Pulse of Life, These Words I Found*

by BA Jorge Alberto Pérez Hernández
Poet, Short-story Writer, Editor, Translator
CCLA Ambassador in Gibara, Cuba
President of the CCLA Sea Dreamers Gibara Group
Editor-in-chief of the CCLA newsletter The Envoy
Contributing Editor of the CCLA magazine The Ambassador

We know Professor Olivé (*Michael* to many friends) for his poems, short stories and original essays. Specifically, we have been witnesses to Professor Olivé´s poetry and his steady growth as a poet. He has written about other authors, so it was about time we wrote about his work. Writing poems and being/becoming a poet are two related yet distinct sides of a coin. Many of us have written at least one poem in our lifetime for various reasons; however, not all of us have stayed on the path, persevered, branched out and *grown* in the "art of writing." He has. He is the CCLA Cuban President, Editor-in-chief of the CCLA magazine *The Ambassador*, Assistant Editor of the CCLA *The Envoy* newsletter, translator, proofreader, poetry anthologies editor and collaborator. He is a member of Holguín University's Department of Canadian Studies and member of the University's Shakespeare Studies Center, in charge of promoting English culture, and member of the Mexican Association of Pedagogues. He is currently involved in many CCLA projects.

He works in the Teacher Education English Department as an Associate Professor of English and English Stylistics. He is the Head of the English Language Discipline. He uses his academic papers, essays, stories and poems in class for reading, debating and practicing the language, adding a didactic and formative element to his scientific and literary production. He also participates in CCLA book donations, presentations and poetry reading in co-curricular campus and community activities.

Olivé's gift blossomed when I introduced him to poet Richard Grove, known as Tai, Founding President of the Canada Cuba Literary Alliance (CCLA), in 2017. Timidly paving his way, he started attending workshops on creative writing with the CCLA, taking valuable advice from Tai and other outstanding poets, like John B. Lee, James Deahl and Antony Di Nardo, reading a lot of poetry, expanding themes and publishing here and there thanks to the generous opportunities Tai offered him.

The process eventually evolved into the presentation of occasional poems, essays and stories in The Envoy (CCLA newsletter); The Ambassador (CCLA magazine); Sea Dreamers issues (Sandcrab Books); a Gibara anthology, *Mis versos son para ti Gibara*, (Hidden Brook Press) dedicated to my town for its 200 years; Introductions to books of poetry, novels and short stories by other Canadian authors (*Some Sort of Normal* (Novel) by Richard Marvin Grove. Hidden Brook Press. 2019; *Redwing*, by Marvin Orbach; *Metamorphosis*, by Graham Ducker; *What Shirley Missed*, by Donna Wootton; *Point Taken*, by Don Gutteridge; *Into a Land of Strangers*, by John B. Lee; etc.)

Then came Bridges Series Book IV, *Where the Heart Lies*, (Hidden Brook Press, 2018) alongside three poets from Canada and Cuba where he published twenty-five poems; and *The Dream The Glory and The Strife*, a 2018 Hidden Brook Press anthology, where he published three short stories and five poems. He has been published too (poetry and essays) in Canadian Stories magazine thanks to James Deahl's support. In early 2020 came his solo full-length, fifty-two-poem book, *Forge of Words*, with HBP too, which I reviewed stating he had "one of the key aspects of poetic craft: individuality. Olivé has successfully found his style – not only in writing but also in reading his poetry before an audience."

Nevertheless, in his opinion, his most significant writing is not poetry but a book with one essay about the CCLA and thirty-five reviews and essays about thirty-one Canadian poets and prose writers, *In a Fragile Moment: A Landscape of Canadian Poetry* (published with HBP in 2020 right after *Forge of Words*), and a second volume he is working on that offers one *emotional* essay on Canada and more than thirty on also over thirty poets and prose writers. Only six poets from the first review book appear here, with new titles.

During 2020 and 2021, he also edited and/or authored books:

The Divinity of Blue. CCLA Visit to Cuba 2020. Hidden Brook Press; *Flying on the Wings of Poetry / Volando en las alas de la poesía.* Hidden Brook Press. 2020; Bridges Series Books, Book V (English-Spanish) *The Heart Upon the Sleeve.* Hidden Brook Press. 2021; *Pedagogical Sciences. The Teaching of Language and Literature, Education, Values, Patrimony and Applied IT.* QuodSermo Publishing. Canada. 2021; *The Light Candling the Mind: Critic and Author in Harmony. Essays and Reviews on Canadian Literature.* QuodSermo Publishing. Canada. 2021; *Five Canadian Poets: Analytical Essays on James Deahl, John B. Lee, Don Gutteridge, Glen Sorestad, A. F. Moritz.* QuodSermo Publishing. 2021; etc.

Olivé was active writing reviews about authors from Canada and Cuba:

"An Essay on Elana Wolff's Poem "Sidewise" in Swoon."; *"Invincibility of Poetry. A Review on Don Gutteridge's Invincible Ink";* *"The Warmest Beat, the Brightest Light on Both Sides of Life's Tunnel,"* on the Canadian anthology, *Hearthbeat. Edited by Don Gutteridge; "Everywhere You Go Beauty Shows,"* on the Canadian anthology *The Beauty of Being Elsewhere. Edited by John B. Lee;* an essay on the book and the poet in *Earth Bound Green Dips to Eternity of Blue. Cuba Poems by Richard Marvin Grove; "A Brief Review on "Extinction," a Poem by Jorge Alberto Pérez Hernández"* and *"A WORD ABOUT Diana Bruzón's Poetry;" "The Slings and Arrows of Outrageous Fortune. A Review on The Blue Dragonfly healing through poetry,"* by Veronica Eley; *"WITH WORDS AND IMAGES WE HOPE. A Review of In Silence We Wait"; "Jorge Alberto Pérez Hernández: One-man Band, Nature and Nurture Poet,"* a review on his book *In my Night Silence;* etc.

As well, he has presented research papers on Canadian studies in scientific events:

8th Scientific Conference WEFLA-SECAN (Canadian Studies). April 2017. "Canada Cuba Literary Alliance Exchanges with the Holguín University Teacher Education English Major Department"; "Marvin Orbach, Merle Amodeo: Canadian Poets, Universal Poets;" "Canada Cuba Literary Alliance Authors: People, Places, Nature and Time." (both in the 9th International Scientific Conference of the Holguín University

(WEFLA) and Canadian Studies International Event. April 2019; WEFLA-SECAN 2021 SEMINAR ON CANADIAN STUDIES. LITERATURE AND CULTURE. "In A Fragile Moment. A Landscape Of Canadian Poetry. A Book Of Reviews And Essays: John B. Lee." April 2021. ISBN; and (Coauthor) WEFLA-SECAN 2021 SEMINAR ON CANADIAN STUDIES. CANADA-CUBA RELATIONS. "Canadian Presence In The Teaching Of Oral Expression In The Preparatory Year At The University Of Havana." April 2021.

I am certain it is relevant to let the public know this because we are reviewing a poet and a poetry book but also, from a broader perspective, his full literary production: his work as an essay writer and as a poet – two intimately connected endeavors – through his relation with poetry as his act of creation and his implicated attitude towards it as his deeper involvement via literary criticism.

About his reviews, Canadian poet and reviewer Ronnie R. Brown said: "… this collection is unique… Prof. Olivé' style may come as a surprise to Canadian readers… However well known or little known, the observations on these works seen by someone "from away" are well worth the read…" Canadian poet and literary expert, James Deahl, called it in different emails "A major study of 31 Canadian poets… This is a critical study of 31 Canadian writers… This is a substantial study... I cannot recall the last time a project of this scope was undertaken. In fact, this book may truly be unique… *In a Fragile Moment*… may truly be unique. I know of nothing like it. Taken together, *Tamaracks* and *Fragile* will put Canuck poetry on the international literary map as never before…"

It is in this context that I have read a digital copy of *This Pulse of Life, These Words I Found*. It is Professor Olivé's second solo book of poems. The new poetic proposal lists eighty-four poems (the *non*-haiku section counted as one). Many of them have been published before, separately, in the issues I mentioned: he justly wanted to condense them – revised and modified – in one volume. There are also brand-new poems. I'd like to think of this poetry book, and invite readers to see it that way too, as a compilation of some of his previous favorite poems and a wonderful complementing set of new ones. Altogether, it is a warm book of "old" (we are talking about poems he wrote and published between 2016 and 2019) and "fresher" poems he wrote from 2019 to 2022.

To date, Olivé has brought to public light more than a hundred poems in a six-year span. His range of themes can be safely – not strictly, as they are oftentimes skillfully blended – organized in this new poetry book in four areas: nature (landscapes, day and night, dawn, the moon, sunset, rain, the sea, storms, birds, etc.); personal, love of family and couple (mother, father, daughter, granddaughter, wife and grandparents); poems to poetry/poets and writing; and general-meditative-religious topics. All of these themes have left easily traceable impressions on his imagery here and in his previous book.

Modesty – he is aware of this and constantly reminds readers – and lyricism as an innermost manifestation of his thoughts and feelings sign this stirring book. The poet, at this point I can call him that despite his reluctance, has been able to go on setting his own bar gradually higher and higher thus improving, boldly improvising and handling words, phrases and linguistic structure in a language that is not his own. And *this alone* is a feat: Olivé is a Cuban Professor, his mother tongue is Spanish! He says he is not a poet, he learned English in college. We may need to keep this in mind, as we may need to be alert at all times that these are *his* poems and this is *his* way to word out feelings. Poets are entitled to their right to voice what they feel. No one can question that.

Reading his poetry, whichever theme, anyone with a heart will have to marvel at the meanings and feelings poured out by the poet in *sui generis* images. There is further evidence in this volume of acute observation of reality and inward exploration. Worldwide poetry he read – particularly British and American but also Latin American – during his senior high and college years, besides Canadian poetry he has been passionately reading the past six years, shows in many of his poems, colored by his romantic appreciation of what surrounds him and leaves a mark on him.

An element of interest is that the poet writes with hardly any direct references to specific events, locations or time. He seems to be intentionally avoiding them, except in some explicit poems which welcome contextualization in space and time. Far from being a flaw, I see it as another signature of his individuality: he ventures into a "nonstop timefulness" we are surprised by in "Daybreak" or an unnamed geography (I venture in saying it is the horizon he can watch from his five-story building porch) in "muse *interruptus* – call": "ridge of jagged hills / blunt/sharp / against the horizon / it punctures the skyline…," a poem ("muse *interruptus* – shower" too) that is highly contemplative *and* suggestive: a description of nature and full sensuousness as we move unsuspectingly into the end.

Another engaging aspect in his poetry is the invariable presence of quotes from British, American, Canadian and Cuban poets, American prose writers, popular British, American and Australian bands and singers, films, and the Bible in all his poems! Olivé takes his readings very seriously and carries their impact next to him, and he is truly willing to let people know how those writers influence him. His input to creative writing overleaps the borders of his critical reviews on poetry and lingers, not only in the poetry he writes but also in these quotations: he quotes more than *fifty* Canadian poets to introduce his poems, which serve him as motivation of his own poems and as a tribute to poets who have inspired his writing. His allegiance to adding quotes to his poems is an admirable one. It also tells us how poets´ thoughts are invisibly connected and mutually inspiring.

My review on *Forge of Words* explained: "From his early works, mostly dedicated to intimate poems to women, to his latest – experiencing all sorts of themes and textual arrangements – it is a joy to witness Miguel's growth as a poet, much of which derives from having read and absorbed fine Canadian poetry during the last three years, and from having followed valuable advice given by poet friends. In reading his book, I became an active witness of things, people and feelings described."

We are impressed by his erotic pieces – which respect limits – evocative and breathtaking; we run for shelter from the rain or feel tempted to be rained on. We sigh with his emotive words to his daughter and his wife, his gentle ways to describe experiences filling his eyes, reaching his mind, and we approve of his reverence at poetry as an act of creation.

As I stated above, there is no absolute thematic separation in the poems. In his previous book I clarified: "… diversity does not affect the palpable cohesion that remains deeply entwined in Miguel's unique style and we sense as we read." His ability goes as far as merging them provoking a trembling sensation of pleasure, allowing free rein to our imagination. Some cases are "muse *interruptus* – call," "muse *interruptus* – shower," as I explained, "Somewhere," with a "galactic," gripping aura: "she holds seeds of pleasure / in her hands / scatters them on my skin

/ gently / softly humming / so they grow / cosmic towards a sun / somewhere in her galaxy," and "Even in the Rain": "Darkening skycanvas looms / beyond the window… // Imminence a thunderbolt away / from bursting into / gusts of rain, / we pause at the sight. / You nudge me and wink / to reclaim the attention you deserve / even in the rain."

He sings to poetry in his opening poem, "complete": "I am zapping words / into my PC screen / can't help it when am inspired / no point in knowing if / it's topnotch or unexceptional material / it just feels good to write," in the sweet-flowing "Dance of Words" and in his stunning "Wingcharm," which is in my view an exploit of language command and a fantastic, dazzling alliance of poetry writing with nature (a bird) during "a millionth of an instant." We cannot tell what reality is "real," what dimension is factual in the fused physical act of writing a poem and a metaphorical "muse" hummingbird (he calls the bird *she*: our representation of the Muses? flapping inspiration for the poet out of its wings.

He chivalrously praises his wife in "Of Your Seasons": "Seasons visit you, quietly. Flowers / you have planted bloom and eventually fade / with the cycles; / but you are always blossoming…" This poem ends with a well-knit erotic finish I won't advance here. Olivé melts in the face of innocence and special love for his daughter in "Silent": "I watch you sleep / I convey thoughts and good wishes / silently let them fly / and perch gently on your hair…," for her and his granddaughter in "Birthdays": "September strums twice / my heart´s strings. Bliss of birthdays / falls like prayed-for rain…" and for the family in his closing poem, "Search": All night I sought for / meanings… / All night, / my wife asleep beside me / next door / my stepdaughter and / my one-year-old step-granddaughter / gently breathe… / on the other side / of Holguín my daughter rests too / in dreams of castles, heroes, fairytales… / These words I found. / The right ones. / The best ones."

In between, remarkable poems like "Your Presence," "Harbinger of Rain," "Tongues of the Ocean," "All in the Day´s Eye," "Almighty, Redemptive," "The Finest Moment" and "The First Day" – this latter poem praised by poet friends like John B. Lee, Richard Grove, James Deahl and Elana Wolff – that call for reflection with an uplifting, steadfast religiousness overflowing their lines. We also find breathtaking photographic pieces like "Visit," impressively compact, syntactically simple ones like his haiku, or "wings of desire," a strikingly sensual poem, or "Collage," "Motif in my Soul," "This summer´s kick," "Rendezvous" and "There," odes to nature, poetry and love.

We perceive a fundamental consistency between many of his pieces. For example, "The First Day": "like the new sun rising / and the sea renewing itself in wavy romance / with the shore / leaving runic signs on the sand, / I breathe in the pulse of life / awake at this hour in the sleepy waterside / I calibrate my existence… / this is where I stand, / before the primordial source. / *God divided light from darkness,* / my eyes receive awakening / this pulse of life refreshed / to embrace me / like *the first day* of all creation" and "Tongues of the Ocean": "Here I stand on the inconstant, undulating line / drawn by the bold tongues of the ocean / soft-lapping the sand, / age-old event remodeler of earth… // a warm wetness / massaging my bare feet / a mind-healing / airborne primeval version of algae, corals fondling / my nostrils…"

There is a confessed purpose in opening-closing the book with "complete" and "Search" respectively. These poems bare his passion for writing and his greatest motivations. Add to this that the lines used, so suitable and eloquent, to entitle the book come from "The First Day": "this pulse of life," and "Search": "These words I found." I am sure no other title could be more opportune than the one chosen by a poet who has strummed life pulses and stimulating words into a book. Feel his pulse, savor his words.

Let the junction overwhelm you as much as it did Canadian professor and poet Antony Di Nardo when he acknowledged: "There are many pleasant surprises in this collection, poems that call to the reader in a voice that is tender, personal, honest, heartfelt and sincere— poems that ask to be heard because Olivé is as much an auditory poet as he is visual." Hear and visualize Olivé´s poetry, dear readers. You won´t be disappointed: variety and substance accompany the lines you will read.

I am proud to have been the agent leading Richard Grove to meeting Olivé. I am more than proud he is showing his true potential beyond frontiers and writes now the way he does. I am happy I was a part of his growth as a poet, prose writer and reviewer, and I take delight in his achievements. He deserves them.

Comments about *This Pulse of Life, These Words I Found*

From the title down every single word used, the poetry book, *This Pulse of Life, These Words I Found* by Cuban Miguel Olivé, is a reflection of a poet who has matured and diversified his poetic proposal. The themes he writes about cover life in its manifold manifestations: love, loss, nature, poetry, family, religion. Depth and feeling, keen observation and passion envelop his wording. I have shivered at his sensuous poems, I have clearly seen the events, phenomena and sights he has photographed in poems for viewers to revel in and never forget – because they will *never* forget.

MSc Marlene Mora
Associate Professor
Foreign Languages Department
University of Holguín, Cuba

I had already read *Forge of Words*, Miguel Olivé's previous solo poetry book published by Hidden Brook Press in 2019. Now he offers this new compilation of eighty-seven poems in his *This Pulse of Life, These Words I Found*, published by Wet Ink Books. Wonderful poems, warm and winning, solid and unforgettable. He is a Cuban poet who writes directly in English then translates into Spanish! I respect that, as I respect his dexterity in the language and his insightful translation of life into poetry. Readers will be moved by themes and poetic composition; they will open their wise eyes – and vulnerable hearts – to a proposal that covers universal themes, like love, penned with his unique style. Read *This Pulse of Life, These Words I Found* by Cuban Miguel Olivé. You won't regret it.

PhD Jorge Ronda
Full Professor
Foreign Languages Department
University of Pedagogical Sciences, Havana, Cuba

This Pulse of Life, These Words I Found, a poetry book by a Cuban professor, Miguel Olivé, enters sweetly through our eyes and sets forever in our minds. The poet's proposal is agile, varied, enrapturing and lyrical. Both short and long pieces are treated with right doses of delicacy and fire, mirroring the poet's understanding of what surrounds him. As he did in his first book (*Forge of Words*, Hidden Brook Press, 2019), Olivé captures reality and feelings, puts them in a poetry furnace and they emerge to impress us and show us our own lives reflected in many of them.

Reading the poetry book *This Pulse of Life, These Words I Found* by Cuban Miguel Olivé made me look back into my life and the way I have faced it. But the look was one of tenderness and appreciation as the poet revealed things I had not noticed and shed a new light upon my own experiences. The book's poetic scope and intent are fulfilled to my pleasure and the pleasure of those who want their hearts to be touched and their bodies to tremble in anticipation and sense of participation in a poet's involvement and ability to reach us. I am grateful I was chosen by Olivé to read his book.

After reading *This Pulse of Life, These Words I Found*, by Cuban Miguel Olivé, your life will change, as will how you deal with every feeling crossing your heart. The poet has a way with words: they reach out and touch you then they settle and give you warmth. Olivé has found the right words to reveal for us how life pulsates.

Acknowledgement of poems previously published

I thank the following sources and formats for their generosity in publishing and/or republishing some of the poems included in this book:

The Envoy, Canada Cuba Literary Alliance digital newsletter. Hidden Brook Press.
The Ambassador, Canada Cuba Literary Alliance official magazine. Hidden Brook Press.
Canadian Stories Magazine. www.canadianstories.net.
Hidden Brook Press:
Solo poetry book (in English and Spanish): *Forge of Words* (2020).
Anthology (in English): *The Divinity of Blue* (2020).
Anthology (in English): *In Silence We Wait* (2021).
SandCrab Books:
Bridges Series Book IV, *Where the Heart Lies* (in English and Spanish) (2018).
Ebook *These Voices Beating in our Hearts: Poems from the Valley* (in English and Spanish) (2020).
Devour Magazine, Art & Lit Canada. Hidden Brook Press.
QuodSermo Publishing:
Five Canadian Poets. Analytical Essays on James Deahl, John B. Lee, Don Gutteridge, Glen Sorestad, A. F. Moritz (in English) (2021).

About the Author

Miguel Ángel Olivé Iglesias is Editor-in-chief of the Canada Cuba Literary Alliance (CCLA) magazine, *The Ambassador*, Assistant Editor of *The Envoy*, the CCLA newsletter, and CCLA President in Cuba. He writes poetry, prose and reviews, does translation, proofreading, reviewing, editing and revision for the CCLA, along with compilation and anthologizing. He is a member of the Mexican Association of Language and Literature Professors, VP of the William Shakespeare Studies Center and member of the Canadian Studies Department of the Holguín University in Cuba.

Born in 1965 in Bayamo, Cuba, he travelled to Holguín City in 1977 for his Junior, Senior High and College studies. Today he is an Associate Professor at the University of Holguín, with a Bachelor's Degree in Education, Major in English, and a Master's Degree in Pedagogical Sciences.

He has been teaching for over thirty years and writing reviews, poems and stories in Spanish and in English. Miguel has written and published numerous academic papers in Cuba, Mexico, Spain and Canada. So far he has published over a hundred poems, four short stories and more than seventy critical reviews of Canadian poetry books and novels in different issues: *The Ambassador*, official flagship of the CCLA; *The Envoy*, official newsletter of the CCLA; The Bridges Series Books, published by Hidden Brook Press and SandCrab Books; Adelaide Group, New York-Lisbon (an essay on a Maltese poet); Canadian Stories Magazine (www.canadianstories.net), and other anthologies by Hidden Brook Press and SandCrab Books.

Hidden Brook Press published his first solo book of poems, in English and Spanish, *Forge of Words* (2019), also an English-Spanish poetry anthology of Holguín poets (an ebook with SandCrab Books) entitled *These Voices Beating in our Hearts: Poems from the Valley*. He is the book´s editor, thirteen of his poems and ten haiku were included too. He also published a book in English with one essay on the CCLA and thirty-five reviews about thirty-one Canadian poets and prose writers, *In a Fragile Moment: A Landscape of Canadian Poetry* (2020).

The author is currently involved in many CCLA projects, which include a second volume of *In a Fragile Moment: A Landscape of Canadian Poetry* (more than thirty reviews on over thirty Canadian poets and prose writers). He works in the Teacher Education English Department as a professor of English and English Stylistics. He is the Head of the English Language Discipline. He continues to use his academic papers, essays, stories and poems in class for reading, debating and practicing the language, adding a didactic and formative element to his scientific and literary production. He also participates in CCLA book donations, presentations and poetry reading in co-curricular on-campus and community activities.